The SPORTS ANSWER BOOK

The SPORTS ANSWER BOOK

Bill Mazer's CHALLENGE ROUND

BILL MAZER

Drawings by BRUCE STARK

PUBLISHERS   *Grosset & Dunlap*   NEW YORK

To my wife, "Dutch"
who allowed me, and I mean
allowed, the luxury of time to myself. If she hadn't, I couldn't have.

Acknowledgment

I would like to express my gratitude to Lud Duroska, indefatigable researcher, enthusiast and sports encyclopedist nonpareil, without whose help and understanding this book would have remained no more than an idea.

Contents

Contents

The
SPORTS ANSWER
BOOK

1

It's Always Open Season

WHERE's the next question coming from?

Ever since NBC began to promote me as "Bill Mazer, the walking sports encyclopedia," I've been fair game for anyone with a question to fire at me.

It reminds me of a movie I saw some time ago called *The Gunfighter*. Gregory Peck, the hero of the story, had the reputation of being the quickest man on the draw. Whenever he arrived in a new town, word would get around about who he was and there would always be an ambitious local gunslinger eager for greater fame and ready to test his prowess against the gunfighter. It's that way with me. Everywhere I go—in a cab, in a restaurant —people try to "gun me down" with sports questions. It keeps me on my toes—and it keeps me happy. And sometimes there's a lot of extra fun when the question and answer becomes a duel. Like this . . .

I go on the air and five minutes later the telephone rings and a voice asks:

"What do you think of Zhabotinsky?"

What do I think of Zhabotinsky? And thousands of people are listening. Zhabotinsky? Just that. No clue even to the sport that goes with the name. Well, I'm not thinking of Zhabotinsky. My memory brings up the image of an old friend, Ken Stoller, a weight-lifter, who got me interested in the sport. If it weren't for this particular friend, I wouldn't have the least notion of who Zhabotinsky was.

My questioner is playing it cute. Okay. I play it his way.

"Well, I like Zhabotinsky. But not as much as Vlasov."

I parry his thrust and the duel is on. Let's see what he does with Vlasov. Just my way of telling him *I know*. And of testing him at the same time.

"Don't you think that Vlasov is over the hill?" he asks, neatly sidestepping.

Still no mention of the sport under discussion. But we're both enjoying this little game, and I hope the radio audience is, too.

"Vlasov has done over twelve hundred," I point out.

"Sure," my questioner counters. "Vlasov is the better quick-lifter, but . . ."

Now he knows that I know and I know that he knows. But what about the listeners? Here's what we were talking about.

Who is the better weight-lifter, Zhabotinsky or Vlasov?

Leonid Zhabotinsky and Yuri Vlasov are two of the best heavyweight weight-lifters in the Soviet Union, where the sport gets considerably more attention than it does in the United States. And being the best in Russia is almost the same as being the best in the world. At least they proved it in the last Olympics in Tokyo.

IT'S ALWAYS OPEN SEASON

Zhabotinsky won the gold medal, lifting 1,259.5 pounds in the three championship categories: the press, snatch, and clean and jerk. This established a new Olympic record. He lifted 478.5 pounds in clean and jerk for a world record, and 368.5 pounds in snatch for a new Olympic mark. Vlasov was not far behind him. He lifted 1,254 pounds to win the silver medal, and he set a world record in the press with 434.5 pounds. Their compatriots did very well, too. Russians finished first or second in five of the other six weight classes. So the musclemen of the rest of the world have their work cut out for them before the next Olympics.

The next call. A lady asks: "What is *roque?*"

I don't even know how to spell it. "Would you believe a cheese?"

Her laugh sets me straight. It wasn't a cheese. All right, lady, you scored a bullseye.

"What is roque? You tell me."

"Well," she says triumphantly, "it's a form of croquet. They got the name for it by dropping the c and t. Roque is played on a clay court instead of grass and the arches are much smaller to make it more difficult to hit the ball through. It's more exciting than croquet and takes more skill. There's even a national association now called the American Roque League which conducts championships each year in two divisions."

Now I know.

The word roque reminds me of *rouge.* "Could you tell me what rouge is? Nothing to do with cosmetics. It's used in pro football."

"I'm afraid I don't know," she replies. Her triumph of a moment ago evaporated.

I feel a little sorry; perhaps I should have told her that

it is a term used only in Canadian football. Then I explain that rouge is a point scored against a team that is unable to return a punt out of its end zone. My victory isn't very sweet. In fact, I feel terrible about it.

Then comes the next call.

A fellow with a British accent asks: "Would you remember when the first international cricket match took place in America?"

That's a stopper.

"I didn't think you would, Bill. It was in 1751, 15 years before the Revolution. New York defeated the team from London, 166 to 130."

"Sounds like an upset."

"More like a preview of what happened in the colonies," my caller replies, chuckling.

Questions about sports have become a way of life with me. They come any time, any place. In the morning I take the train into the city and I sit quietly, staring out of the window, preoccupied with thoughts about my radio program. The guy sitting next to me has a few ideas of his own.

"Know anything about boxing?" he asks suddenly.

"Know anything about boxing? I don't even know you." Of course, I smile when I say this. Weakly.

My answer doesn't faze him. He's not even listening.

"What was Benny Leonard's real name? How about Jack Bernstein? Battling Siki? Jack Sharkey? Vince Dundee? Johnny Dundee? Ted 'Kid' Lewis? Willie Pep?"

He didn't wait for my answers. And a good thing, too. These were mostly old timers and a few, at least, I was sure to miss out on.

"Benny Leonard's name was Benny Leiner; Jack Bern-

WHAT'S IN A NAME?

stein was John Dodick, and he wasn't Jewish. Battling Siki was Louis Phall, Jack Sharkey was John Cucoshay, Vince Dundee was Vincent Lazzaro and Johnny Dundee was Joseph Carrora. Gershon Mendeloff became Ted 'Kid' Lewis when he went into the ring and Willie Pep's name was William Papeleo."

That wasn't the end of his questions and answers. The guy talked a mile a minute, racing the train into New York. And I have to admit I enjoyed the role of a listener for a change.

Walking to the RCA building, I thought about the old-time fighters, how they so often changed their names and how and why different nationalities seemed to take turns

15

being on top in boxing—the Irish, the Jews, the Poles, the Italians, and in recent years, Negroes and Puerto Ricans.

Many times I've been asked, "What makes a good fighter?"

Once I answered without thinking:

"Poverty."

I think that's the real answer. Boxing offers them a chance to get out of the slums, earn economic security, achieve prestige or, as some put it, "gain status." Yes, poverty is the spur. Did you ever hear of a millionaire's son becoming a club fighter—or battering his way to a championship?

But I said it's always open season and I've got to expect the unexpected. It came as I entered the NBC lobby. A man stopped me and introduced himself.

"Do you consider archery a sport?"

"Oh, yes."

"How about hunting with a bow and arrow?"

"I think better of that than hunting with a gun. Personally, I'd rather hunt with a camera. I don't like killing animals for sport."

"Well, here's a question for you. What's the biggest animal ever killed with a bow and arrow?"

I didn't really know the answer. But I knew the elephant was about as big as they come on land. So I answered quickly, "An elephant."

The man smiled wryly. "That wasn't a hard question."

"No. I guessed."

"You guessed right. A man named Howard Hill brought down an elephant that weighed five tons. It was in East Africa back in 1950."

"Now it's my turn to challenge you. What kind of arrow did he use?"

16

"It was a 41-inch one and the bow had a 120-pound pull."

That's how it is. I slipped his punches and came out the winner by a decision. I entered the elevator and a man nods and smiles.

"You're Bill Mazer, aren't you? I wonder if you ever heard of Hiram Connibear?"

I reach back to my college days.

"Wasn't he the famous rowing coach at the University of Washington? He developed a stroke that made his crews so outstanding that they were national champions for many years."

"That's right," he acknowledged, and he seemed very pleased that I knew of Hiram Connibear.

I remembered reading an article recently about American coaches switching to a European-designed oar. Its different shape meant a change in the stroking technique Connibear had perfected. I wondered if the man knew that and, if he did, whether it bothered him that his old idol was being overshadowed by changing developments in the sport.

I finally reach my office, but there's no escape from questions. My secretary grins, mischievously.

"Bill, I'll bet you don't know the sport of Sphairistike."

"Write it down. I certainly don't know it from the way you're pronouncing the word."

This gave me a minute to reflect. Just recently she had started playing tennis and I had seen her with a book on the sport.

I picked up the slip of paper on which she had written down the name, frowned convincingly, and said, "Sphairistike, that must be the original name of tennis."

"You're right," she said, not happy about it.

I have to admit to luck. Lefty Gomez, when he was pitching for the Yankees, used to say, "I'd rather be lucky than good." I agree with him.

But she wasn't through yet.

"How about the name of the man who invented the word?"

"Now wait a minute. Enough is enough."

"You're stumped," she said, triumphantly. "He was an English officer, a Major Walter Wingfield."

"Thinking up a word like that! I'll bet he could never make it writing advertising copy." Secretaries are the hardest people in the world to impress. I slumped into my chair and muttered, "I hope they court-martialed the Major."

Before I can start on my mail, my boss, George Skinner, walks in. He admits to knowing nothing about sports. So naturally he has a question.

"Who is My Own Brucie?"

"A rock-and-roll singer?"

"No."

"Then he's a handsome cocker spaniel who won best in show at Westminster not once, but twice. In 1940 and 1941."

My Own Brucie must have been tremendous. In the dog world, Westminster is like the World Series or the U. S. Open in golf. And winning back-to-back is really rare.

Skinner walks away satisfied. Well, happiness is being able to live up to your boss's expectations.

And so I take up my mail. A Newark, New Jersey, listener writes in to disagree, vehemently and at great length, as to who is the better ballplayer, Mickey Mantle or Willie Mays. This has been one of the most frequently asked questions over the past few years. Since it is an opinion question, there is absolutely no way to prove who is right and who is wrong.

Who is the better ballplayer, Mickey Mantle or Willie Mays?

Mays and Mantle are the two great centerfielders of our time. Mickey is the more impressive physically. As a power hitter his credentials cannot be challenged. After all, he has come closest to belting a fair ball out of Yankee Stadium when one of his prodigious wallops reached the façade of the third deck in dead right field. He has to his credit the longest measured home run, and it has been fairly well verified. Against the Senators, in

April, 1953, Mickey rapped one at Griffith Stadium which traveled 565 feet and, of course, he has had many other "tape-measure" hits. His multitude of injuries—which prevented Mickey from achieving fully his tremendous potential—made him one of the great inspirational leaders baseball has ever known. The effect on the other Yankees when he is in the line-up cannot be measured by any tape yet invented. He plays on sheer "guts," and usually in pain.

And yet, when you consider performance on the basis of the better all-around player, my vote goes to Willie Mays. I think Mays is more the complete player. You can forget, or take into account, the fact that he shares the distinction along with Ruth, Foxx, Williams and Ott of hitting more than 500 home runs. Or that he presently stands second only to Ruth in the total number of homers. You might forget that he is an exceptional base runner, that he has one of the great throwing arms of all time. His glove alone would make him a candidate for the Hall of Fame. His peerless defensive ability completely tips the scales in his balance. That's the way I see it. Each can have days when he puts on a performance that will make you gasp and say, "No greater player ever lived!" But I think Willie Mays will have more such days.

Here's a long letter from a regular listener, a nice guy who earns his living washing windows. In the midst of a number of personal observations and some welcome compliments, he throws in a question.

"What National League umpire has the same name as a former defenseman on the Canadiens who became a player-coach for the Rangers?"

On the margin of the letter I jot down: Doug Harvey.

Another letter, from a bowling enthusiast, asks:

IT'S ALWAYS OPEN SEASON

Why did bowling change from a nine-pin to a 10-pin sport?

It seems that in the middle 1800's bowling was strictly a nine-pin game, growing in popularity in the Eastern area, particularly New York and Connecticut. Unfortunately, disreputable elements entered the scene and the gamblers and hustlers gave the sport an unsavory reputation. The situation was thought to be so bad that Connecticut passed a state law banning "nine-pin bowling." To circumvent the law, somebody added the extra pin making it a ten-pin game. It caught on. Eventually, the American Bowling Congress was organized in 1895 and brought respectability to the sport. The ABC standardized alleys, equipment and rules and built the foundations for what has probably become America's most popular family-participation sport.

More letters, more questions.

What was Connie Mack's real name? Cornelius McGillicuddy.

What National League player hit the most doubles? Stan Musial.

Who was the third baseman in the famous Tinker-to-Evers-to-Chance infield? Harry Steinfeldt.

Who succeeded Babe Ruth in right field for the Yankees? George Selkirk.

I go through my mail—some of it—and then it's time to go on the air. The fans will be ready to shoot their questions at me. I know the phones are already busy. I know some of my listeners have been sharpening their questions for the *Challenge Round* a long time.

I go on the air and five minutes later the telephone rings and a voice asks:

"Do you know Nancy Hanks?"

"Abraham Lincoln's mother?"

"I don't know about that. The Nancy Hanks I'm talking about is in sports."

"Well, that *was* the name of Lincoln's mother."

"What sport was she in?" the voice asks, laughing.

Bill Mazer's been shot down.

"Nancy Hanks was a trotter who set the first record in the two-wheeled sulky, back in 1892."

"Okay, you got me," I admit.

And that's what it's like. You'd think the sports fans who think up all these questions are some kind of nuts. Maybe they are. Maybe I am, too. They're wonderful people. I love the game of wits and the constant challenge and the never-ending fun of it. And thank God for that strange quirk in human nature, the never-satisfied hunger to ask questions. Maybe they're not world-shaking questions. But they are the spice of life.

2

The Real Swingers

"THE Ruth is mighty and shall prevail."

That was the brilliant opening sentence of a story written one afternoon in the Yankee Stadium pressbox by Heywood Broun, then a baseball reporter and later to become a famous columnist. He had just watched Babe Ruth put on a typical performance and demolish the visiting team with a few swings of his bat.

And when the greatest home-run slugger in history retired, it was thought that his record of 60 homers in a season would surely prevail. And it did for 34 years. Then along came Roger Maris. It's ironic the record breaker was Maris. One would have expected Mickey Mantle. But it was Maris.

Before Maris only two of the many other fine long-ball hitters had managed to come close to Ruth's record through the years.

Which two players came closest to breaking Ruth's home run record before Maris?

In 1932 Jimmy Foxx of the Philadelphia Athletics banged out 58 and in 1938 Hank Greenberg of the Detroit Tigers belted the same number. But Foxx got his 58th on the last day of the season. Greenberg's case was more frustrating. The Tiger batsmith walloped No. 58 with five games still to play . . . and then he was shut out the rest of the way.

By the way, did you know that someone has hit 59 home runs in one season? Oh, you knew the Babe had done that too. Okay.

A lot of fans are reluctant to concede that Maris broke Ruth's record because he played in 162 games and the Babe made his mark in a 154-game season in 1927. Commissioner Ford Frick said at the time that Maris' record would go into the books with an asterisk to denote the difference in the length of seasons. But Maris' feat doesn't deserve to be minimized. For one simple reason. How many realize that Maris actually came to the plate only *six* more times than Ruth, 698 to 692! That total includes all times at bat, counting walks, sacrifices and being hit by a pitched ball. Since Ruth was walked more often, Maris ended up with 50 more official at bats, 590 to 540 for the Babe.

You might not remember that Tom Zachary of the Washington Senators threw home run ball number 60 to Ruth, but Maris' feat should be fresher in your mind. Can you recall those last few exciting days in 1961 when Maris was making his bid for immortality?

Who was the victim of Maris' 60th homer? Of his 61st?

Maris connected for number 60 off Jack Fisher of the Baltimore Orioles in the third inning of a night game at Yankee Stadium on Tuesday, September 26, 1961. According to one veteran observer, John Drebinger of *The New York Times*, Maris' homer landed about 40 feet to the right of Babe's 60th in the right-field bleachers.

Maris elected to sit out the next game on Wednesday to try to rest from the heavy publicity and other pressures that had made his record-try so nerve-wracking. The following day was a regularly scheduled day off, leaving Roger with a three-game weekend series against the Boston Red Sox for the now-or-never 61st.

Bill Monbouquette started for Boston on Friday night and blanked Maris in four confrontations, although he walked him twice. On Saturday afternoon Don Schwall muffled Maris' thunder, getting by with a walk and a single in four at bats in the next-to-last game.

Tracy Stallard, a rookie right-hander, took the mound for Boston on Sunday. He got Maris to fly out in the first inning. In the fourth Roger was up again. The first two pitches were balls. Stallard then fired a fast ball over the plate and Maris smacked it into the right-field box seats, creating baseball history.

There was a fierce struggle for the ball by the expectant fans. For the last three games they had packed the right-field stands waiting for this moment. And it was not all baseball sentiment. A Sacramento, California, restaurant owner had offered $5,000 for the ball Maris hit. A young Brooklyn truck driver got it. His prize included an all-expense-paid honeymoon trip to Sacramento to receive the $5,000.

Lost in the tumult—not that it mattered much, since the Yankees had already clinched the pennant—was the fact that the homer was the only run and had won the game. Maris also gained an extra dividend since it was his 142nd run batted in and enabled him to beat out Jim Gentile of the Baltimore Orioles for the RBI crown by one run!

If it's any consolation to Ruth's admirers, the Babe outhit Maris on the season, batting .356 to .269 for Roger.

Incidentally, I think it's perfectly legitimate to compare two players who are both still active and have been around long enough to have had good and bad years, like Mantle and Mays. It's comparing players from different eras that I don't like. How can anyone, really, compare Maris and Ruth, or Maury Wills and Ty Cobb, without cancelling out their argument with qualifications of time and place and over-all condition of the sport. Go on comparing your active favorites, it's great fun and at least you're comparing living, breathing human beings and not two opposing columns of figures. Remember, this game of baseball, and for that matter any game, is made up of people competing against real live people who are on the same field or court or track with them. That's what it's all about, the here and now.

Babe Ruth, who had a lifetime batting average of .342, once said in an immodest moment that if he had wanted to go for singles instead of homers, he would have batted .600. He was probably right, too. One of the reasons he was a great hitter was his remarkable eyesight. They tell the story of Babe being able to read the label of a 78 r.p.m. record while it was revolving on the phonograph— not the slow-moving modern 33 and 45 r.p.m. long-playing records, but the old-fashioned standard record. If you want to appreciate how difficult it is, try it.

In the next generation, Ted Williams had the reputation of having the keenest eyes as well as the quickest reflexes of any ball player who ever lived. The Boston Red Sox batting stylist could delay his swing longer than other players because he could follow the ball until it was practically in the catcher's mitt and still whip his bat around in time to connect. He was said to be able to see the bat and ball make contact!

Williams prided himself on his knowledge of the strike zone. He refused to swing at a pitch even an inch or two outside the zone. He probably missed out on a lot of base hits, but he made more than his share, as witness his career batting average of .344, two points above the Babe on the all-time list. The Splendid Splinter also is likely to be the last major-leaguer to bat over .400. One reason is all the night games, the constant jet-plane travel from coast-to-coast and the changing time zones that play havoc with a player's physical condition.

29

What year did Williams hit over .400 and what was his average?

Williams turned the trick in 1941 when he batted .406. It should be noted that he refused to play it safe on the last day of the season. He was hitting .401 and could have sat out a double-header to insure staying above the rare .400 mark. But he insisted on playing—and made six hits to raise the average to .406.

Harry Heilmann of the Detroit Tigers was the last previous American League .400 batter with a mark of .403 in 1923.

Bill Terry of the New York Giants was the last National Leaguer to accomplish the feat with a .401 average in 1930.

Here's a teaser:

What batting honor did Babe Ruth, Willie Mays, Stan Musial and Joe DiMaggio fail to achieve?

None of them ever won the triple crown! And they have lots of company. Few have been able to do it. The combination of having the highest batting average, the most home runs and the most runs batted in in your league requires consistency and power at the plate—and the right circumstances, since any other player enjoying a standout year in one of the categories can knock you out of contention.

So it's understandable that only ten players have won the triple crown. But what's amazing is that two of them were able to win it twice!

THE REAL SWINGERS

Who were the two players who won batting's triple crown twice?

Rogers Hornsby of the St. Louis Cardinals swept the board for the first time in 1922, hitting 42 homers and batting in 152 runs with a .401 average. He repeated in 1925 with 39 homers, 143 RBI's, and a .403 average.

Ted Williams wrapped up his first triple crown in 1942 with 36 home runs, 137 runs batted in, and an average of .356. He won his second in 1947, batting .343 as he stroked 32 four-baggers and drove in 114 runs.

Who were the other eight players who won batting's triple crown?

Ty Cobb of the Detroit Tigers was the first triple-crown winner in 1909. He hit .377, batted in 115 runs and topped the league in homers with the grand total of nine. Heinie Zimmerman of the Chicago Cubs was the next in 1912 with 14 homers, 98 RBI's and an average of .372.

After Hornsby's "double," two Philadelphia stars, Jimmy Foxx of the A's and Chuck Klein of the Phillies, made a clean sweep in the same year, 1933. Foxx batted .356, drove in 163 runs and rapped 48 four-baggers. Klein had 28 homers and 120 runs batted in with a .368 mark. Lou Gehrig followed the next year, with credentials of 49 homers, 165 RBI's and a .363 average. Joe ("Ducky Wucky") Medwick of the St. Louis Cardinals had a banner season in 1937, getting 31 homers (tying him with Mel Ott of the Giants) and 154 runs batted in with a .374 average. Next was Mickey Mantle of the Yankees in 1956.

31

He had 52 homers, 130 RBI's and a .353 average. And in 1966 Frank Robinson of the Orioles had 49 homers, 122 RBI's and a .316 average.

Which great hitter holds the National League record for the most batting titles won in a row?

Rogers Hornsby compiled the most astounding streak as he led the league for six straight seasons from 1920 to 1925. Look at the figures: .370, .397, .401, .384, .424 and .403! For the last four seasons he had an average of .403 and for the six-year span he averaged nearly .397! In all he won seven titles, one less than the recordholder, Honus Wagner.

Hornsby also set an example of dedication to his trade not easily equaled. Zealously guarding his eyesight, the Rajah refused to indulge himself in the pleasure of attending the movies. He believed—rightly or wrongly—that watching the "flickers" would harm his eyes. I wonder if a modern-day player would make a similar sacrifice, like refusing to watch the in-flight movie between Los Angeles and New York, or turning in at eleven and not staying up to watch a tape of his last interview with the press corps. I guess he might if he were to enter the record books with the highest lifetime batting average of any right-handed hitter, as Hornsby did with a mark of .358.

Who has the highest lifetime batting average as a left-handed hitter?

Ty Cobb, who led the American League 12 times, posted a career mark of .367, including averages of .420 in 1910 and .410 in 1911. Cobb was undoubtedly one of the flashiest players the game has ever seen—and also one of

the brassiest. It's some indication of the diversity of baseball that he shares a niche in the Hall of Fame and a page in the record books with one of the quietest, gentlest, most self-effacing athletes who ever lived—Lou Gehrig.

Lou Gehrig, the Yankees' "Iron Man," had the misfortune to play in the shadow of Babe Ruth for most of his playing career. But there is one hitting department in which he surpassed the Babe and all other hitters.

What home-run record does the Yankees' Lou Gehrig hold?

In the matter of walloping homers with the bases loaded, Gehrig had no peer. He clouted 23 grand-slammers in his career. The closest to him are Jimmy Foxx and Ted Williams, with 17 each. The Babe hit a total of 16.

Speaking of grand-slam home runs:

Which two players on the same team hit grand-slammers in the same inning?

Bob Allison and Harmon Killebrew of the Minnesota Twins connected with the bases full against the Cleveland Indians on July 18, 1962, at Bloomington, Minnesota.

Who holds the record for consecutive grand-slam homers?

Jim Gentile of the Baltimore Orioles walloped two in the first and second innings on May 9, 1961.

The grand-slammer is the biggest blast a hitter can get (except maybe signing up to do a razor-blade commercial), but *any* home run is a big thing for a player, and very few of them will complain about how and when it was achieved. But there is an exclusive breed who make it a habit of hitting multiple homers in single games. The ultimate achievement is four, and here's a challenge question:

34

THE REAL SWINGERS

Only nine players have ever hit four home runs in a single game. Who were they?

This exclusive list starts back on May 30, 1894, with Robert Lowe of Boston, who remains the only National Leaguer to clout his four in consecutive times at bat. Ed Delahanty of Philadelphia was the next four-in-a-game hitter on July 13, 1896. Then it took almost 36 years before Lou Gehrig did it on June 3, 1932, against the Athletics in his first four trips to the plate. Gehrig nearly became the only player to wallop five, but Al Simmons raced deep into left field to haul down his long drive in the ninth inning.

Chuck Klein joined the group on July 10, 1936, although he needed ten innings to do it. Twelve years later Pat Seerey of the Chicago White Sox performed the deed on July 18, 1948, and he needed 11 innings. Gil Hodges of the Brooklyn Dodgers was next on August 31, 1950. Joe Adcock of the Milwaukee Braves rapped his four on July 31, 1954. Rocky Colavito of the Cleveland Indians followed suit on June 10, 1959, and Willie Mays of the San Francisco Giants was the last player to do it on April 30, 1961.

An interesting sidelight is that Billy Loes was a spectator at the last four four-homers-in-a-game feats, either on the same team as the hitter or on the opposing team!

More uncommon than belting four homers in one game is smashing two grand-slammers in one contest. It's happened only five times, four times in the American League.

Who are the five players who hit two grand-slam home runs in one game?

Tony ("Poosh 'Em Up") Lazzeri of the New York Yankees was the first to hit for the circuit twice with the bases filled, on May 24, 1936. Jim Tabor of the Boston Red Sox was next, clouting his two four-run specials to celebrate the 4th of July in 1939. Seven years later another Red Sox

slugger, Rudy York, did it on July 27, 1946. The last
American Leaguer was Jim Gentile of the Baltimore Orioles who cleared the bases twice on May 9, 1961.

This leaves one National Leaguer and you should remember him since it happened during the 1966 season. Yes, it's Tony Cloninger, who became the first National Leaguer through all the years to perform the exploit—and a pitcher, to boot! The Atlanta Braves' righthander made Bob Priddy and Ray Sadecki of the San Francisco Giants his victims in that order. In the same game he also singled in a ninth run that established a major-league record for most runs batted in in one game by a pitcher.

In the good old days (for pitchers) of the dead ball, the home run was not considered much of an offensive weapon; the bunt, the stolen base, the hit-and-run were the most effective plays and consequently were what players concentrated on most. It was not until the era of "Home Run" Baker of the Philadelphia Athletics that the four-bagger became popular with the fans and, subsequently, with the players.

Home Run Baker got his nickname for obvious reasons, but he certainly wasn't the present-day fan's idea of a slugger.

What were the most home runs Home Run Baker ever hit in one season?

Would you believe 12? That's the number. Baker was the home-run leader in the American League in 1911, 1912, and 1913, and his respective totals were 9, 10 and 12. His lifetime total was 93!

Speaking of sluggers of the pre-live-ball era, there was one who hit .400 in his rookie year! Rookies are usually good hitters or they wouldn't be given the chance to break in in the first place, but this feat was phenomenal, dead ball *or* live ball.

THE REAL SWINGERS

Which player in his first full season, officially considered a rookie, batted over .400?

Shoeless Joe Jackson, after playing a total of 30 games in three previous seasons, became a regular outfielder for the Cleveland Indians in 1911 and he swatted the ball for a .408 average!

Jackson, who posted the third highest lifetime batting average (.356), was such a natural hitter that, although he was one of the Chicago White Sox players found guilty of conspiring to "throw" the 1919 World Series to the Cincinnati Reds, he still batted .375 in the Series!

The classic poignant line "Say it ain't so, Joe" was supposed to have been said by a youngster who, with tears streaming down his face, approached the great hitter after the news had broken about the Series conspiracy.

These days rule changes come pretty slowly, about as slowly as changes in the United States Constitution (even slower, to judge by the raft of Supreme Court decisions we've had lately), but in the old days they didn't have such a reverence for the rule book, often changing it to suit their own needs. Here's a far-out question about rule changes.

In 1887, a change in the rules enabled three players to hit over .400. What was the change in rules and who were the players?

During the 1887 season—and that season only—a batter was allowed four strikes instead of three, and bases on balls were counted as hits! Come to think of it, it's a wonder that only three players hit the .400 mark. That ball really must have been dead!

The players who received this unprecedented boost to their averages and reached the magic mark were Cap Anson of Chicago (.421), Dan Brouthers of Detroit (.419), and Sam Thompson of Detroit and Philadelphia (.406). If they ever revived that rule change we'd have to put a time limit on games, as in basketball—and the scores of the two games would probably be about the same!

They had some pretty high averages in those days, but in some years everybody just seemed to lay off the ball. As witness the following question.

What were the lowest averages ever needed to win batting titles in both leagues?

Elmer Flick of Cleveland hit a mere .306 in 1905 to cop American League honors and Larry Doyle of the New York Giants led the National League in 1915 with a .320 mark. Those must have been great years for pitchers!

In 1941 Joe DiMaggio embarked on one of baseball's most notable batting feats—his hitting streak that extended through 56 consecutive games. He started his fantastic splurge on May 15 in a game against the Chicago White Sox when he singled off pitcher Edgar Smith.

Who stopped Joe DiMaggio's 56-game hitting streak?

Actually, three men conspired to stop DiMaggio's hitting streak during a night game in Cleveland on July 17, 1941. They were the starting pitcher, Al Smith, relief pitcher Jim Bagby, Jr., and third baseman Ken Keltner. Keltner was the real hero—or villain, if you prefer. He

CELTS	10	16	22	17	23	
GIANTS					31	16

deftly handled two hot smashes down the line that were ticketed for hits and turned them into outs.

A measure of how Olympian a record DiMaggio set is the fact that the best previous consecutive-game hitting streak was compiled back in 1897 when Wee Willie ("Hit 'Em Where They Ain't") Keeler batted safely in 44 straight contests.

Which player dominates the all-time batting categories in the National League?

Stan ("The Man") Musial. He is first in number of at bats (10,972), runs (1,949), hits (3,630), doubles (725), total bases (6,134), and runs batted in (1,951). He is third in singles (2,253), seventh in triples (177), and fourth in home runs (475).

I also have no problem remembering how old Musial is —since he was born 19 days after I was.

Which active player has the highest lifetime batting average?

If you guessed Willie Mays, you guessed wrong—he's second best with a .314 average. Hank Aaron, who in my opinion is one of the greatly underestimated players of his generation, is the pace-setter. He has averaged .320 for his first 12 years in the majors. I think he's frequently overlooked when rating present-day players because he's not flamboyant—just does his job quietly and efficiently. Nobody gets wood on the ball as often as Aaron does, and he has power, too. (He had 398 homers at the start of the 1966 season.) A great player who deserves more accolades.

Who holds the record for the most runs batted in in one season?

Lewis Robert ("Hack") Wilson of the Chicago Cubs, who propelled 190 runs across the plate in 1930. Lou

Gehrig owns the American League mark of 184 set in 1931.

Who holds the record for the most base hits in one season?

George Sisler of the old St. Louis Browns, who banged out 257 safeties in 1920.

Who holds the record for the most extra-base hits?

No, not Babe Ruth. Stan Musial is the man, with a total of 1,377 (725 doubles, 177 triples, 475 homers). Not that the Babe was far behind—he had a total of 1,356.

Who has hit the most home runs over a short span of time?

Ralph Kiner, of the Pittsburgh Pirates and now of the New York Mets' broadcasting team, had a sizzling bat for three days back in 1947. From September 10th to 12th he smacked eight home runs in four games.

And so it goes. But most of this is of interest only to the statisticians. What interests me most is the great hit, the timely hit, the hit that wins a game. If it happens to have been made by one of the immortals of the record book, all fine and good. But what intrigues me is the hit by the unknown or little known player who blasts his way to fame, but not immortality, with one stroke of the bat.

Perhaps the statisticians are right, perhaps it is only in the long run that a great hitter proves himself, but they can't convince me of that when it's two down in the top of the ninth and the manager waves down to the bullpen for a pinch hitter and out comes . . . My god! It's—

3

The Well-Armed Men

Down through the years, from Cy Young to Sandy Koufax, there have been many great pitchers. And during my time some of the best were active, and I was lucky enough to have seen most of them. It's funny how you sometimes don't appreciate them. Take Carl Hubbell, for example. I didn't appreciate him then. I should have. I was witness to two of the greatest performances this man ever gave. But as a youngster I was a Brooklyn Dodger fan—a devout Dodger fan. And Hubbell pitched for the arch-enemy—the New York Giants.

Hubbell, the master of the screwball, was a tall, quiet lefthander who reminded me of Gary Cooper—he had that same kind of serious dedication. That quality was never more apparent than on a Sunday afternoon, July 2, 1933. I'll never forget that day if I live to be a hundred. It was at the Polo Grounds, home of the enemy, and there I was—from eight o'clock in the morning to eight that night. The early arrival at the ballpark was the penalty for being able to afford only a bleacher seat. But the wait **was** certainly worth it. That double-header for sheer pitching has to be the greatest you could ask for. The Cardinals and Giants were fighting for the league lead. I can still remember the line-ups. St. Louis had Rip Collins, Frankie Frisch, Leo Durocher and Pepper Martin in the infield, Joe Medwick, Ernie Orsatti and Ethan Allen in the outfield, and Jim Wilson catching. The Giants' regulars **were** Bill Terry at first, Hughie Critz at second, Blondy Ryan **at** short and Johnny Vergez at third. In the outfield were Joe

("Jo-Jo") Moore, Lefty O'Doul and Mel Ott, and Gus Mancuso was behind the plate.

Hubbell and Tex Carleton started the first game. King Carl was really king that afternoon. He mowed down the Cards inning after inning. They never got more than one hit an inning off him and the closest they came to scoring, I remember, was when Frisch belted a couple of line drives that were nearly home runs. Carleton also was in superb form and the two dueled into extra innings . . . 13th, 14th, 15th. Finally Carleton tired and Jess Haines took over on the mound for St. Louis.

Hubbell, however, continued to be invincible, in his methodical manner thwarting the Cards' batters. At last the Giants broke through in the 18th. Jo-Jo Moore walked and got to third on a sacrifice and a groundout. A moment later Critz lined a single to right-center and King Carl had a richly deserved 1–0 triumph.

Hubbell had hurled a six-hitter and had set down the Cardinals in order in 12 of the 18 innings. And he didn't allow a walk! What a masterpiece of a game, all 4 hours and 3 minutes of it.

. But there was more to come. As if inspired by the pitching exhibition in the opener, LeRoy Parmelee and Dizzy Dean put on another sterling show in the second game. Dean was being called on by manager Frisch with only one day's rest to get the Cards even—and he almost proved equal to the task. But Parmelee stilled the Cards' thunder for nine innings, doling out four safeties, and walked off with a 1–0 victory in the semi-darkness. Vergez' homer in the fourth inning produced the only run as Dean gave up just five hits.

The double shutout boosted the Giants' lead to 5½ games and they were on the track to the pennant.

A little more than a year later, July 10, 1934, to be exact, I was at the Polo Grounds to watch the 1934 All-Star game and my special hero, Van Lingle Mungo, rather than Hubbell. As fate would have it, Mungo pitched only one inning, the fifth, and much to my embarrassment—and I guess his, too—he was raked for six runs by the American League sluggers. But before Mungo arrived on the scene, Hubbell put on as dazzling a pitching exhibition against those same feared hitters as has ever been seen.

What feat did Carl Hubbell accomplish in the 1934 All-Star game?

Hubbell struck out the side in both the first and second innings. But what makes it really remarkable is that among his victims were Babe Ruth, Lou Gehrig, and Jimmy Foxx! A "murderers' row" if ever there was one!

There was no hint of the superlative feat to come in the way in which Hubbell started. Charlie Gehringer opened the game with a sharp single. Hubbell then walked Heinie Manush. Two men on, none out, and Babe Ruth at the plate! Hubbell and the National League cause were in trouble. But undismayed, the Giants' southpaw put all he had on his pitches, using mostly the screwball, and fanned the Babe on three pitches. Lou Gehrig was next. He went down swinging. Jimmy Foxx then dug in at the plate and became the third strikeout victim. Did that Polo Grounds crowd roar!

In the second inning Al Simmons led off for the American League and he whiffed. Joe Cronin stepped in and Hubbell notched his fifth strikeout. Bill Dickey then broke the spell and lined a single. Lefty Gomez, admittedly not much of a hitter even for a pitcher, quickly became strikeout No. 6 as Hubbell wrapped up the finest two innings of mound work in All-Star history.

What two records involving streaks does Carl Hubbell hold?

In the 1933 season Hubbell set the National League record for the most consecutive scoreless innings—46⅓. (Walter Johnson holds the American League record with 56, which he posted in 1913.) Interestingly enough, Hubbell's 18-inning 1–0 victory over the Cardinals, which set a National League mark for pitching the longest shutout game in the modern era, was not part of the consecutive scoreless streak.

His other record is the highest number of consecutive victories over two seasons. He finished the 1936 season with 16 in a row (he won 26 in all that year) and started the 1937 campaign with eight straight for an over-all total of 24.

Far different from Hubbell in temperament but the same in talent was a contemporary, Jerome Herman ("Dizzy") Dean, the talkative, colorful, hard-throwing right-hander for the St. Louis Cardinals.

Until a 1937 All-Star incident, when Earl Averill's line drive broke Dizzy's toe, causing him to use an unnatural pitching motion and harm his arm, he had all the equipment and confidence to become one of the greats of baseball.

Not one to be modest, Dean loved to boast of his ability, but he usually was able to back up his bragging. There is his classic spring prediction in 1934 that "Me and Paul [his brother] will win 45 games," a statement widely hooted at. But the Dean brothers delivered.

THE WELL-ARMED MEN

How many games did each of the Dean brothers actually win during the 1934 season?

Dizzy racked up 30 victories—and nobody since has been able to match that total—and Paul contributed 19, which made a total of four more than Dizzy had predicted! Usually forgotten is that the Dean boys had another tremendous season the next year, with Dizzy winning 28 and Paul 19, a total of only two fewer than in 1934.

The anecdotes about a carefree and self-assured character like Dizzy Dean are many. There's the one about the time he is supposed to have told the Braves before a game in Boston that he wouldn't throw any curves that day, just fast balls. He kept his word and not only beat them, but shut them out!

Another I like was his remark after a doubleheader against the Dodgers in September of 1934. Diz pitched the first game and held Brooklyn hitless for seven innings. Meanwhile, the Cards had bombed the Dodgers' staff and had run up a 13–0 lead. Easing up, Diz allowed two meaningless singles in the eighth and one in the ninth for a very creditable three-hitter. Paul pitched the nightcap and turned in a no-hitter.

What was Dizzy's reaction?

"If Paul had told me he was going to pitch a no-hitter," he joked, "then I would have pitched one, too!"

Back in the mid-thirties, the ban against Negro players was still in effect, of course, in organized baseball but that didn't prevent major-leaguers from going on barnstorming tours after the season was over and playing against a picked team of Negroes. Dizzy went on one tour and hooked up in many pitching duels with Satchel Paige, who only got to the majors in the twilight of his career more than a decade later. (But old Satch's twilight was one of the longest on record.)

Although born on a farm in Arkansas, Dizzy was not color-blind to ability. Asked after the tour whether Paige, considered the finest Negro hurler at the time, could have made it in the big-leagues, Dizzy answered:

"Why, if Satch and I were on the same ballclub, we'd have the pennant clinched by the Fourth of July and we could go fishing until the World Series!"

And now for some pitching questions. Here's an easy one about one of my favorites:

Who is the winningest left-hander in major-league history?

It's Warren Spahn, and he chalked up 363 triumphs in 21 seasons. There have been lefthanders who threw harder and those who had better breaking stuff but there is no one who made better use of his talent or went about his trade more intelligently. He was a great improviser. When his fast ball started to lose a little of its zip, he improved his curve ball. When he needed another breaking pitch, he learned to throw the screwball. He was a thorough craftsman on the mound and he had a fierce desire to win. He's a cinch to be elected to the Hall of Fame as soon as he's eligible—and rightly so.

What other major-league record does Warren Spahn hold?

He won 20 or more games a season more years than any other lefthander—12.

What modern pitcher has hurled no-hitters in both leagues?

Jim Bunning. He pitched his first for the Detroit Tigers against the Boston Red Sox on July 20, 1958, and then when he went to the Philadelphia Phils in 1964, he threw his second no-hitter against the New York Mets on June 21, 1964, and made it a perfect game, too.

What famous turn-of-the-century pitcher was the first to post no-hitters in both leagues?

Denton ("Cy") Young, who pitched for Cleveland and no-hit Cincinnati in the National League on Sept. 18, 1897, and then repeated in a Boston uniform against Philadelphia in the American League on May 5, 1904. And his second no-hitter was a perfect game! He added a third no-hitter against the Yankees on June 30, 1908. As yet, he and Bunning are the only two pitchers to have pitched no-hitters in both leagues.

At one time it looked as though Bobby Feller was going to dominate the pitching record books, but along came World War II and robbed him of three full seasons—when he was in his prime as a pitcher. But you certainly have to admit that he made a good start!

What is unique about Bobby Feller's first no-hitter?

Feller threw the only no-hitter ever pitched on an opening day when he burned his fast ball past the Chicago White Sox on April 16, 1940, for a 1–0 victory for the Cleveland Indians. This is about the only distinction left to Feller, since in 1965 Sandy Koufax breezed past his record of 348 strikeouts in one season, raising it to 382. But to those of us who saw him, Feller remains one of the great pitchers of all time. And don't forget that wartime layoff when he was busy with the Navy on more urgent matters.

Koufax now rules the roost in the no-hit column, but there are still many no-hit games worth remembering:

What is unique about Alva ("Bobo") Holloman's 1953 no-hitter?

Holloman's no-hitter is the only one ever pitched by a rookie making his first major-league start. Holloman handcuffed the Philadelphia Athletics on May 6, 1953, for the

St. Louis Browns. Despite his spectacular debut, however, Holloman didn't linger in the majors very long. Before the end of his first and last season in the big leagues he had been farmed out.

What was especially significant about Allie Reynolds' second no-hitter of the 1951 season?

It's the only one ever pitched on the final day of the season, but it has a greater significance—it clinched a pennant! The Yankees were playing a doubleheader with the Red Sox at Yankee Stadium on September 28 and needed a victory to take the pennant. Reynolds came through in spades. It's the game you might remember where Yogi Berra dropped a pop foul off the bat of Ted Williams for the final out, forcing Reynolds to get Williams "out" twice.

Who pitched the only two consecutive no-hitters and who were the opposing teams?

Johnny Vander Meer of the Cincinnati Reds performed the double no-hit feat, the lefthander blazing his fast ball against the Boston Bees on June 11, 1938, and four days later throttling the Brooklyn Dodgers in the first night game at Ebbets Field.

Who pitched the longest no-hitter?

Harvey Haddix of the Pittsburgh Pirates joined the list of all-time hard-luck pitchers on the night of May 26, 1959, when he mowed down the Milwaukee Braves one,

two, three for 12 innings. The first Braves' hitter in the 13th got on on an error, and after a sacrifice and an intentional walk, Joe Adcock's double turned the no-hitter into a one-hit 1–0 defeat.

What was unusual about Fred Toney's 10-inning no-hitter against the Chicago Cubs for the Cincinnati Reds in 1917?

For nine innings Toney's mound opponent, Jim Vaughn, also hurled a no-hitter! The only time in the majors when there were two no-hitters going in the same game. After one out in the 10th, the Reds finally got a hit off Vaughn and scored the winning run.

Who has hurled the most no-hitters?

Sandy Koufax with four. The Los Angeles Dodgers' brilliant southpaw posted his first against the New York Mets on June 30, 1962. His second was on May 11, 1963, against the Giants. The third was on June 4, 1964, against the Phillies. The record-breaking fourth was on September 10, 1965, against the Chicago Cubs.

There is still one no-hit record that Koufax has not yet tied, let alone broken, and that is pitching two no-hit games in one season. As we've seen, Johnny Vander Meer and Allie Reynolds both turned the trick, but there was one other pitcher who managed it.

Who is the only pitcher besides Vander Meer and Reynolds to hurl two no-hitters in one season?

Virgil Trucks of the Detroit Tigers, who stopped the Washington Senators on May 15, 1952, and the New York Yankees on August 25 of the same year.

To end this discussion of no-hitters and no-hit games, here's a pushover:

THE WELL-ARMED MEN

What do Grover Cleveland Alexander, Lefty Grove, Early Wynn and Robin Roberts have in common?

These are as illustrious careers as the world of baseball has even seen, and yet not one of these men ever pitched a no-hitter in the major leagues. And to these names we'll probably soon have to add another—Whitey Ford. Yes,

LIKE COOL, MAN— REAL COOL !

impossible as it may seem, Whitey has never pitched a no-hitter in the majors. Well, you can't have everything, although Whitey comes pretty close to having it all. And anyway, his career isn't over yet, and he may surprise us all and pull one out. If he does, it will probably be the "coolest" game ever pitched.

To round out this chapter and to make sure that not *all* of your favorites (players and questions) are slighted, here are some random challenges:

What is Hub Pruett best remembered for?

Certainly not his pitching record. He bounced around the majors for parts of seven seasons between 1922 and 1932 with four different clubs, never winning more than seven games in any season. His record was mediocre—he won 29 games in all and lost 48. But if he didn't bother most hitters, he had the Indian sign on one: Babe Ruth. A lefthander whose best pitch was a curve, he had phenomenal success against Ruth during his three seasons with the St. Louis Browns. The Babe was glad to see Pruett move to the other league.

What rookie pitcher won the most games?

Grover Cleveland Alexander donned his first big-league uniform with the Philadelphia Phils in 1911 and impressed from the start, compiling 28 victories in his freshman year.

THE WELL-ARMED MEN

How many games did Sandy Koufax win in his first six seasons?

Like a young Dodger hurler several years before him—
Rex Barney—Koufax had blinding speed and limitless
potential when he joined the Dodgers in 1955. Barney
never did get his control problem solved. Sandy seemed
headed for the same fate. He had a lackluster 36–40 record to show for his first six seasons. Catcher Norm Sherry
helped put Sandy on the right track by telling him that he
needed to throw only half as hard as he did to become a
big winner. In 1961 Sandy began to win consistently—he
won 18 games—and the rest is history.

A pitcher's ERA—his earned-run average—is considered a more reliable indicator of his effectiveness than his
won-lost record, which depends to a large extent on how
much batting and fielding support he receives from his
teammates.

How do you figure out a pitcher's ERA?

If a pitcher has an ERA of 1.00, for example, it means
that he has allowed an average of one earned run for
every nine innings he has pitched. To determine the ERA,
divide the total number of innings pitched by nine. Then
divide that figure into the total number of earned runs
charged to the pitcher. In batting, a .300 or higher average
is rated very good. The equivalent in pitching is an ERA
of 3.50 or lower.

Who is the all-time major-league leader in lowest earned-run average among pitchers who have won more than 200 games?

Grover Cleveland Alexander takes the honors with an ERA of 2.56 for 696 games. The American League leaders are Bob ("Lefty") Grove and Hal Newhouser, tied at 3.06.

THE WELL-ARMED MEN

*Who still holds the season record for the lowest
earned-run average for a lefthander in the
American League?*

None other than Babe Ruth, who had an ERA of 1.75
for 324 innings in 1916. In the National League Carl
Hubbell is the recordholder with a 1.66 ERA in 1933.

Who holds the record for the most strikeouts?

Walter ("Big Train") Johnson of the Washington Senators fanned the grand total of 3,497 batters. The record
for a lefthander is held by Warren Spahn who whiffed
2,583 hitters during his career.

*Who holds the record in each league for retiring the most
batters in a row?*

Harvey Haddix of the Pittsburgh Pirates ran up a streak
of 38, the last 36 of whom were put out in order during
the 12 innings of the May 26, 1959, night game against the
Milwaukee Braves when he went on to lose his no-hitter—
and the game to boot—in the 13th inning.

In the American League Vic Raschi of the New York
Yankees set the record of 32 during the 1950 season.

*Who holds the record for pitching the most years in the
major-leagues?*

The record is 23 years and it's shared by John Quinn
and Early Wynn. Quinn, a right-hander, started in 1909
with the New York Yankees and then pitched for the
Boston Braves, Baltimore of the Federal League, the Chi-

cago White Sox, the Yankees again, the Boston Red Sox, the Philadelphia Athletics, the Brooklyn Dodgers, and finished with the Cincinnati Reds in 1933. He posted a 247–216 won-lost mark.

Wynn did less traveling between ballclubs during his lengthy stay in the majors, playing only for the Washington Senators, the Cleveland Indians and the Chicago White Sox from 1939 to 1963. He scored 300 victories and lost 244 games. You might remember what a tough time he had in his final season to get that last precious triumph that put him in the exclusive 300-game winners' club.

Which pitcher was tagged for the most grand-slam homers in his career?

The doubtful distinction goes to Bob Feller who was the victim of bases-loaded four-baggers eight times.

Which pitcher holds the record for the most home runs allowed?

The champion "gopher-ball" thrower is Robin Roberts who had given up 487 homers going into the 1966 season.

What is the record number of runs given up in one game by a pitcher?

Thirty-five! The hapless thrower was Dave Rowe of Cleveland and his disastrous afternoon was way back on July 24, 1882. I guess the team was short on relief pitchers.

THE WELL-ARMED MEN

Which pitcher has led the league in earned-run average the most number of times?

Bob ("Lefty") Grove was the American League leader nine times, five seasons with the Philadelphia Athletics and four with the Boston Red Sox.

Which pitcher holds the record for the most one-hitters?

Bob Feller was only one away from a no-hitter in 12 games.

Who has pitched the most shutouts?

Walter Johnson blanked the opposing team in 113 games.

What record did Sandy Koufax establish in 1963?

Koufax hurled 11 shutouts for the Dodgers that year, the most in one season by a lefthander.

Which pitcher has issued the most walks?

Early Wynn, who gave 1,775 bases on balls.

Who tied Bob Feller's strikeout record of 18 in one game?

Sandy Koufax struck out 18 Giants in September of 1959 to equal Feller's record. He did it again against the Cubs three seasons later.

The hottest conversation piece on my program has been one question, and I might as well repeat it here to end this chapter:

Who is the better pitcher, Koufax or Marichal?

I have maintained that if I were a manager and had to win one game there's only one man I'd use. He's from Brooklyn . . . he's lefthanded . . . and he throws bullets. The Marichal fans always counter by telling me that Koufax has only two pitches while Marichal has as many varieties as Heinz. Well, let's just put it this way, Walter Johnson needed only one pitch to win over 400 games. And anyway, with those two pitches of his Sandy has set records that are incredible. As a matter of fact, that word "incredible" just about sums up this young man whose sense of responsibility added to his obvious athletic talents makes him one of the most unusual athletes of all time.

4

Pennants in Overtime

"RALPH BRANCA says you don't know much about sports."

How would you like to be on the air and have somebody throw that at you?

The youngster, still excited by the whole incident, was telling me—and the listeners—about meeting Ralph Branca the other day. Just like fans of all ages, he had been thrilled to shake hands and have a conversation with a one-time major-league star. He was enthusiastically recounting what was said, and mentioned that he had brought my name up on an opinion-type question and told Branca, "That's what Bill Mazer says."

And Branca retorted: "What does he know about sports?"

Embarrassment . . . chagrin . . . annoyance . . . a lot of emotions and thoughts went through me. Here I had been broadcasting in New York just a few months, after 16 years in Buffalo, and I was trying to establish myself in the metropolitan area. And here was a star on some great

Brooklyn Dodger teams, my old favorites, throwing a curve at me!

I let a couple of seconds go by. They seemed like an hour. My first experience in such a situation and I didn't really know how to handle it. I swung from the heels:

"I may not know much about sports, but I do know who threw the home-run ball to Bobby Thomson in the 1951 Dodgers-Giants playoff."

It was unkind, I'll admit, but I wasn't in a benevolent mood.

Later on when I met Ralph, he told me that he'd only been kidding. I know him now and I know he was kidding, but it took my knowing him to realize it.

But now that I consider it, it must be kind of rough for a guy who broke into the majors when he was only eighteen and stayed up there for 13 seasons to be best remembered for one poor pitch rather than for all his good games (he won 21 in 1947) and for two World Series performances.

Maybe you know that Branca was the victim in one of baseball's most memorable episodes. But how much else do you recall about the players and the events leading up to Thomson's dramatic ninth-inning wallop?

Most of us swore we'd never forget any detail of that inning. I mean that was our generation's equivalent of Ruth's called home run, or the long count in the Dempsey-Tunney title fight of 1927. But time takes its toll and not too many of us are the total recall types who stand around waiting for some quiz show to recognize real talent when they see it. Furthermore, a whole new generation, or maybe three or four generations—they come around a lot faster than when I was a kid—have made the scene since then and they themselves have quite a few

69

memorable moments to forget—or, more likely, to retain, to stump me with.

Anyway, whether or not you were on the scene that mighty autumn afternoon ("when they put him in the ground"—to paraphrase the rest of Emily Dickinson's famous line) you probably know that Branca was the hapless pitcher who served up the biggest gopher ball of all time. But what else do you remember?

How many runs were scored in the last half of the ninth inning of the 1951 Dodgers-Giants pennant playoff series?

Four. Now let's relive that inning.

The Dodgers were ahead, 4–1, as the last half of the ninth inning started at the Polo Grounds in that third and deciding game of the 1951 playoffs. It seemed to be all over for the Giants. Don Newcombe was pitching for Brooklyn and the big righthander had been burning 'em in all afternoon. The Giants had only four hits through eight innings and Newk showed no signs of weakening.

The first man up was Alvin Dark. He got an infield hit. When Don ("Mandrake") Mueller singled, putting runners on first and third, the Giant fans started roaring. Monte Irvin quieted things by popping out. But Whitey Lockman banged out a double, driving in Dark and making the score 4–2. On the play Mueller sprained his ankle sliding into third and had to be carried off the field. Clint Hartung (the "Hondo Hurricane," remember?) went in as a pinch runner.

Dodger manager Chuck Dressen then made the fateful decision. He called in Branca from the bullpen. (After the game Dressen unkindly attributed the choice of the reliever to his bullpen coach.) Thompson was waiting at the plate. After his warm-up pitches, Branca fired a strike past Thomson. On the next pitch, the Scot from Staten Island connected. There was no doubt about it. The ball soared into the lower left-field stands for a three-run homer, a 5–4 victory and the National League pennant.

In pitching to Thomson instead of walking him and setting up possible double plays all around the infield, Dressen was going by the book: Never put the winning run on base.

Maybe the Dodgers should have walked Thomson. The next batter was a rookie. Although the rookie outfielder had stardom written all over him, he was having a miserable playoff series, with only one safety in ten at bats. But then again maybe he was overdue for a hit. His name? Willie Mays.

An added historical item: Only two days before, in the first playoff game at Ebbets Field, Thomson smacked a homer good for two runs that sent the Giants on to a 3–1 triumph. And can you guess who the Brooklyn pitcher was? That's right. Ralph Branca.

Baseball history doesn't repeat itself exactly, but while we're on National League playoff series, consider the parallels of the 1962 playoffs with the 1951. The same clubs, the same team winning out, except that the 1951 payoff game ended with a bang and the 1962 one on a less dramatic note.

The pennant races were similar, with the Giants whittling away at what appeared to be a safe Dodger lead in the closing, hectic weeks and finally tying for first place on the final day. And the playoffs followed the same script on the West Coast. The Giants took the first tussle and the Dodgers the second. The third game was a carbon copy, too, with the Dodgers in front, 4–2, as the Giants batted for the last time in the ninth.

PENNANTS IN OVERTIME

Who was on the mound at the start of the last inning of the last game of 1962 Giants-Dodgers playoff?

Trying to lock up the flag for the Dodgers was Ed Roebuck, pitching in relief for the sixth time in seven days. He had been the big "saver" during the season, racking up ten straight before finally losing one late in the campaign. Called in in the sixth, the Los Angeles righthander had squelched a Giants' threat without giving up a run. Now it was the ninth and he had a two-run lead.

Matty Alou opened the Giants' last stand with a single, but he was forced at second by Harvey Kuenn. Then Roebuck faltered. Willie McCovey walked. So did Felipe Alou, loading the bases. The ducks were on the pond—as Red Barber used to say—and the Dodger fans at the Coliseum were restive. Willie Mays smashed a line drive off Roebuck's hand and Kuenn easily scored. The Giants were only one run down.

That was all for a tired Roebuck, and Stan Williams took over. Orlando Cepeda flied out, bringing in the tying run. Two out and Ed Bailey up. Williams wild-pitched Mays to second, so Bailey was intentionally walked. The bases were full again. Jim Davenport strode to the plate and, without swinging once, drove in the winning run! Williams' control had completely deserted him. Davenport just had to stand there as Williams walked him on four straight pitches, forcing in Felipe Alou from third with the important run. After the Giants scored again on an error, the Dodgers submitted meekly in order in their last at-bats and so the Giants were playoff champions again, this time by a 6–4 score.

PENNANTS IN OVERTIME

What distinction do the Dodgers have when it comes to pennant playoffs?

The Dodgers have one distinction when it comes to playoffs for a pennant. Whether in Brooklyn or in Los Angeles, they have been involved in all four post-season series in the history of the National League.

The first—and also the first in the majors—was in 1946 when the Dodgers and the Cardinals ended in a flat-footed tie after the last day of the regular campaign. Both clubs blew a chance to win it without going into overtime when they lost their final games, Mort Cooper of the Braves shutting out the Dodgers, 4–0, and the Cubs beating the Cards, 8–3. The St. Louis players had more reason to kick themselves, since they had faltered in the last few days, dropping three of their last six starts.

The Cards got back on the track in the playoffs, taking two straight despite the frantic manipulations of Brooklyn's leader, Leo Durocher, who used five pitchers in the first contest and six in the second to no avail. Eddie Dyer, the St. Louis pilot, had much better luck with his hurlers. How much do you recall about the first playoff series in baseball?

Who were the two winning pitchers for the Cards in the 1946 National League pennant playoff?

Howie Pollet and Murry Dickson. Pollet earned the hero's laurels in the opening game at St. Louis on October 1, 1946, by scattering eight Brooklyn hits and walking off with a 4–2 triumph. The crucial victory was also the left-hander's 21st of the season (performances in the playoffs count in the regular-season statistics). The only Dodger to bother Pollet was Howie Schultz, who platooned with Ed Stevens at first that year. Schultz smacked a solo homer in the third and batted in the other Brooklyn run with a single in the seventh.

The first losing pitcher in a playoff was a fellow who ran into even tougher luck in another playoff series we've already talked about. Yes, it was Ralph Branca. After giving up a run in the first, Branca was knocked out of the box in the third as the Cards scored twice—but he almost got out of the inning unscored upon. With one out Stan Musial walked and Enos Slaughter singled him to third. Whitey Kurowski then grounded into a potential inning-ending double play but he beat the relay to first and Musial scored on the play. Joe Garagiola, who wasn't as bad a hitter as he pretends in his stories on the air, and Harry Walker followed with singles for another run and Branca departed in favor of Kirby Higbe, trailing 3–1.

The Dodgers had a threat going in the seventh as Schultz knocked in their second run, but Slaughter's fine peg from right cut down Bruce Edwards at third and killed off the bid.

The Cards then gave Pollet an insurance run in their half of the seventh on Musial's triple and Garagiola's one-bagger, but the St. Louis southpaw didn't need it as he shut the door the rest of the way.

Speaking of Garagiola, who figured large in that playoff game, I always pronounce his name with the hard "g" (Gara-GO-la) when I'm kidding him, because that's how we used to know him—in our ignorance or innocence, I can't say which—when he first broke in with the Cardinals. Now that he's a well-known announcer and pulling down more loot than a corporation lawyer, I defer to his

AN' A BIG HELLO TO YOU FANS OUT THERE.....

JOSEPH GARAGIOLA, ESQ.

exalted position and pronounce his name with the soft "g" (Gara-JEE-ola). I guess Joe's soft "g" is equivalent to the "Mr." we are awarded before our name when we're promoted out of the mailroom. Joe's made it big, and without losing that celebrated sense of humor and self-deprecating air that made him the toast of the winter-smoker season, but I still sort of miss seeing him behind that plate. Nowadays about the only plate you're likely to see him behind is a blueplate. (Sorry about that, Joe.)

When the second game of the series opened two days later (there weren't any jets around in those days), 31,-437 of the Brooklyn faithful were at Ebbets Field to see if their boys could square matters. But they had little to cheer about as the Cardinals unlimbered a 13-hit attack against more than half of Durocher's mound corps. Joe Hatten was tagged for five runs and he failed to get beyond the fifth inning. Musial's double and Slaughter's triple were the big blows in chasing Hatten to the showers.

While the Cards were piling up an 8–1 lead through eight innings amid the increasing gloom in the stands, Murry Dickson was puzzling the Dodgers with his right-handed slants, allowing only two safeties.

Then, in their last stand in the ninth, the Dodgers raised some flickering hopes by routing Dickson. Augie Galan opened with a double. After the redoubtable Dixie Walker flied out, Ed Stevens tripled and Carl Furillo singled. Two runs were in and Dickson lost his "cool," as the saving goes now. With Pee Wee Reese up, he let loose a wild pitch and then walked the Brooklyn shortstop. Dyer waved in Harry ("The Cat") Brecheen, the crafty lefthander. He proved equal to the task, but not until he dug the hole a little deeper.

Edwards singled, bringing in Furillo and making the score 8–4. When Brecheen walked Cookie Lavagetto, filling the bases, the Brooklyn partisans raised the roof, anticipating a miracle finish. But it was not to be. Brecheen curled a third strike past Stanky, and Schultz, batting for Dick Whitman, took three mighty swings, hoping without success to make it a new ballgame, and the Dodgers were dead.

After suffering through the traumatic 1951 playoff experience, the Dodgers, now in Los Angeles, found themselves in their third overtime series in 1959. At last the outcome was to be happier. Their opponent was the Milwaukee Braves as the two clubs beat out the San Francisco Giants in a hot stretch scramble and deadlocked for first place. Let's see what you can recall about this playoff series.

Who were the two standouts in the first game of the 1959 Dodgers-Braves pennant playoff?

The Dodger rookie Larry Sherry, who had been called up in midseason, starred in the opening game at County Stadium on September 28. He relieved Danny McDevitt in the second inning with one out, one run in and two Braves on base. An error by Maury Wills and a forceout gave Milwaukee its second tally. Sherry then shut the Braves out the rest of the contest, yielding only four hits.

The Dodgers tied the score at 2–2 in the third on one-base hits by Charley Neal, Norm Larker and Gil Hodges off Carl Willey. John Roseboro, the other star of the day, then whacked a home run to open the sixth and that completed the scoring as the Dodgers won, 3–2.

The next afternoon at Memorial Coliseum the Dodgers pulled out the second game in 12 innings, 6–5, to become the National League champions. This time the Braves were the victims of a ninth-inning uprising. Lew Burdette,

a 21-game winner that year, had spun a fine seven-hitter and went into the last frame with a 5–2 edge when the Los Angeles bats come to life.

Wally Moon, Duke Snider and Hodges rapped Burdette for consecutive singles to start the ninth. Manager Fred Haney then yanked Burdette, who wasn't used to being the goat, for Don McMahon, his No. 1 fireman.

Larker belted a two-run single and McMahon was relieved by Warren Spahn. Furillo's sacrifice fly brought in
Hodges with the tying run. Joey Jay finished out the
inning with the Dodgers unable to score again and the
game became the first and only extra-inning playoff contest. The Dodger breakthrough in the 12th, with Bob
Rush pitching, started with Hodges walking and going to
second on Joe Pignatano's single. Furillo hit a high
bouncer over the middle that Felix Mantilla, playing only
because Johnny Logan had been injured in the seventh,
grabbed behind second. The future Met then threw
wildly to first and Hodges raced home with the deciding
run.

The winning pitcher, by the way, was Stan Williams,
who held the Braves hitless over the last three innings. A
relief hero in this playoff series, he was to be a goat in the
next.

While the National League and the Dodgers have had
four post-season series, the American League has gotten
itself into only one overtime situation—in 1948—when the
Cleveland Indians and the Boston Red Sox finished in a
dead-heat for first-place honors. The Indians faltered in
the closing week and fell back into the tie when Hal
Newhouser hung up victory No. 21 as the Detroit Tigers
shelled Bob Feller and beat Cleveland, 7–1, on the final
day. In catching up to the Indians, the Red Sox wiped out
the Yankees' flag hopes on the last two days with 5–1 and
10–5 trouncings.

Deciding not to follow in the senior league's footsteps
with a two-of-three series, the American League settled
on one game to determine the pennant-winner. Boston
won the coin toss and the playoff was held on a cool
Monday afternoon, October 4, at Fenway Park before

81

33,957 fans, who were hoping that the Red Sox would make the World Series an all-Boston affair for the first time in Series history. How much do you recall of the only A.L. playoff contest?

Who were the batting and pitching stars in the 1948
  Cleveland–Red Sox playoff?

To the chagrin of the Boston rooters, the game proved
to be one-sided, with not even their great Ted Williams
putting on a passable performance. The Indians' peerless
playing leader, Lou Boudreau, was the prime executioner
at bat, and Gene Bearden, a 27-year-old rookie southpaw,
scuttled the Boston attack by hurling a five-hitter.

Boudreau, who batted .355 for the season, went 4-for-4,
crashing two homers and a pair of singles. Joe McCarthy,
in his first year as Boston manager, picked Denny Galehouse to start and the Cleveland manager teed off for his
first four-bagger in the opening inning. In the fourth,
Galehouse left the scene after Ken Keltner slugged a
three-run homer and Ellis Kinder came in. Boudreau's
eighteenth clout of the season in the fifth made the score
6–1 and the Indians went on to an 8–3 victory.

Bobby Doerr's 27th homer with one on in the sixth was
the only damaging blow for the Red Sox as Bearden
stayed in command and joined the 20-game winners'
circle.

Ted Williams was held to a single in four at bats and
muffed a fly ball, letting in a run in the eighth, for a
lackluster effort.

Although not a playoff game, a replay of a highly controversial game in 1908 with the pennant at stake properly
belongs in this chapter, in my opinion. I'm referring to the
Giants-Cubs contest when Fred Merkle's "boner" in fail-
ing to touch second base resulted in a tie and forced the
replay after the season, which the Cubs won. Merkle forever after has been cast, unjustifiably, I think, as the

biggest bonehead in baseball and the man who cost the Giants a pennant.

Who was the Cub player who spotted Merkle's "boner," forcing the Giants-Cubs replay of 1908?

You couldn't ask for a more dramatic situation for one of baseball's biggest rhubarbs. The Cubs had swept a double-header the day before with Mordecai ("Three-Finger") Brown winning the first in relief and the second as a route-going starter. That put Chicago six percentage points behind the Giants going into the famous September 23 game. The teams were tied, 1-1, with two out in the last of the ninth. Moose McCormick was on third and Merkle on first when Al Bridwell lined a clean single to center. McCormick ran home with what seemed to be the winning run, the fans at the Polo Grounds rushed on the field, and Merkle, having seen McCormick cross the plate, neglected to tag second and started running toward the clubhouse in centerfield.

But Johnny Evers, the fiery and brainy Chicago second baseman, hollered for the ball in the milling crowd, touched second base, claiming a forceout, and umpire Hank O'Day concurred, ruling the run didn't count.

Why is it so unfair to call it Merkle's "boner" all through the years? Because what he did was the *custom* in those days. Players were in the habit of running off the field once the winning run had scored rather than proceeding to the next base. Merkle was guilty only of doing what the other players were in the habit of doing. He hadn't been careless or forgetful. And only the quick-witted Evers had realized that the practice was a breach of the rules.

In fact, the umpires were so accustomed to this situation that earlier in the month Evers had made the same play against the Pirates and the umpire (ironically it was O'Day) had ruled against Evers! Only later did O'Day recognize that the Cubs' star had been right in his interpretation of the rules and, fortunately for the Cubs, O'Day was on hand to uphold Evers against the Giants.

Another interesting note is that there are several con-

flicting versions as to whether Evers got the right ball to make the force. One version is that Art Hofman, the centerfielder, threw the ball in to Evers. Another is that Iron Man Joe McGinnity of the Giants flung the ball into the stands and that a Chicago sub, hearing Evers yell for the ball, threw him a spare one from the sidelines!

John McGraw, the Giants' blustery manager, ranted at the umpires but the decision stood. The game should have continued into the 10th inning, but play was impossible with all the fans on the field and the umps declared it a tie. This gave Frank Chance, the Cubs' manager, the opportunity to put in a squawk that Chicago deserved a 9–0 forfeit victory because it was up to the home team to keep the crowd under control.

Harry Pulliam, the president of the National League, upheld the umpires' decision and said the game would be replayed the day after the season ended. McGraw then appealed to the league's board of directors, who concurred with Pulliam.

The rest was anti-climactic. The Cubs eliminated the Pirates from contention and finished in a tie with the Giants. The immortal Christy Mathewson, who had already won the unbelievable total of 37 games, was well rested for the key game, but the Cubs, led by Joe Tinker —who hit Matty as if he owned him, as the phrase goes— chased Matty and finished with a 4–2 victory behind Jack Pfeister.

Years later McGraw admitted that it was not Merkle's "boner," and that Evers' shrewdness should be credited for the incident. But fact seldom catches up with legend, and Merkle, who actually was a smart and aggressive player, never was able to live down the "bonehead" appellation.

Merkle's not the only player who's gotten a raw deal from posterity, nor will he be the last as long as people tend to forget the actual play or game and retreat into the half world of statistics or legend or prejudice. I sometimes feel that the game (and I, for that matter) would be better off if the fans concentrated all their powers (and some of them are phenomenal) on what actually happened in the great games and not what statistical coups were counted. Quite a few reputations would be cleared or revived, and quite a few statistical strawmen would be exposed.

5

The Clutch Performers

A PHENOMENON known as "World Series fever" sweeps across the country every fall. Casual fans who devoted little attention to how the teams were faring during the season and seldom saw a game, even on television, succumb come the first of October. They read the sports sections avidly, memorizing batting averages and won-lost records. At the first opening they are ready to debate the merits of the two league champions: Who can hit the long ball, who has the better defense, the more reliable bullpen. They chip in on "runs" pools and make side bets. The custom of the "Series siesta" flourishes as they duck out of the office to watch the game on TV or, if they can't get away from the job, keep an ear to the radio. No other sporting event captures the imagination and attention of the public as does the Series. Despite the great spurt in popularity of pro football, for one week baseball is truly the national pastime.

Would you believe that because of the Series and its hold on Americans a revolution was once delayed?

Back in 1914 Pancho Villa was a Mexican bandit general. (Maybe you've seen *Pancho Villa* on the Late Late Show, with Wallace Beery's colorful portrayal of the rebel leader.) Villa had assembled his troops and was preparing to battle the Mexican army and take over the government. He happened to be publicity conscious, which is

why he permitted an American newspaperman, John Reed, in his camp. He wanted the United States to learn of his exploits. Everything was in readiness for the attack. But Reed pointed out to Villa that if he wanted to be in the headlines in America, he would have to postpone his revolution for a few days. The Series was on and Reed convinced Villa that he could not push the Series off the front pages. Villa did wait (until the "Miracle" Braves swept the Athletics, 4–0), and then gave the word for the revolution to begin.

The history of the World Series is so rich with dramatic incidents and memorable plays that it's difficult to decide which one to start with. My choice is the 1932 Series when Babe Ruth "called" his home run against the Chicago Cubs in the third game. Never did a player put himself on a bigger spot than the Babe did when he majestically pointed to the centerfield bleachers and then made good on his reckless gesture by walloping the ball right to where he had indicated. How well do you know the circumstances surrounding the Babe's rash "call"?

Why was the 1932 Yankees-Cubs Series such a bitter one, goading Ruth into "calling" his homer?

The Cubs infuriated the Yankees when they voted only a half-share to Mark Koenig, who had been called up by Chicago in mid-season and had filled in at shortstop, hitting .353 and playing a key role in the Cubs' drive to the pennant. Koenig had been a popular Yankee for several seasons in the late twenties and his old teammates were incensed at what they considered to be miserly treatment of the ex-Yankee. With Ruth in the lead, the Yankees taunted the Cubs from the start. (Incidentally, the announcement of how the players have split their shares has since been put off until after the Series is over.) The Cubs returned insult for insult and the choice epithets flying back and forth undoubtedly set a high for a Series.

The Yankees won the first two games at Yankee Stadium before the scene shifted to Wrigley Field. In the third game Ruth homered his first time up, but the Cubs rallied to tie the score, and it was 4–4 when the Babe came to bat in the fifth. The Cubs' bench unleashed a torrent of abuse, and the hometown fans, chagrined at the pounding their favorites had been taking, joined in the heckling of the Yankee slugger.

Charley Root was pitching for Chicago. He threw a strike past Ruth and the jeers grew louder. The Babe disdainfully gestured with his bat toward centerfield. Another strike zipped in. The boos and catcalls reached a higher crescendo. The Babe wordlessly pointed to the bleachers again so that no one could mistake his meaning.

Root wound up and threw. Ruth swung. The ball went sailing into the center-field bleachers, just where he had pointed to. The Babe had done it!

The rest of the Series was anti-climactic. The Cubs' spirit was broken. They lost the game, 7–5, and they lost the next one on the following day to make it four in a row for the Bombers from the Bronx.

And this, his most famous Series home run—his 15th— proved to be the last one Ruth ever hit in the postseason classics.

An historical note: Because of his flamboyant deed, Ruth obscured the feats of Lou Gehrig, who seemingly was always destined to play in the Babe's shadow. The Yankees' Iron Man was the star batsman of the Series,

with three homers and a sizzling .529 batting average. Yet it was still Ruth's Series.

Another mighty blow, with the Yankees on the receiving end this time, was struck in the fourth game of the 1947 Series by a Brooklyn Dodger. It ruined the closest bid for the first no-hitter in Series history up to that time.

Who was the pitcher who nearly threw a no-hitter in the 1947 Yankees-Dodgers World Series?

Floyd Bevens was the Yankee pitcher who came so close to baseball immortality. Although he had been wild, putting himself in trouble often, Bevens had silenced the Brooklyn bats for eight innings. Two of the many bases on balls he issued had paved the way for a Brooklyn run in the fifth. The Yankees, however, had scored twice so that Bevens was protecting a 2–1 lead as well as striving for the no-hitter as the last of the ninth opened.

Bruce Edwards, the leadoff batter, flied out. Bevens then gave up his ninth walk, to Carl Furillo. Spider Jorgensen popped out in foul territory to George McQuinn. Only one out to go! But Al Gionfriddo, a pinch runner for Furillo, swiped second, running as Brooklyn had throughout the Series on Yogi Berra, who was then inexperienced behind the plate. Pete Reiser, who had an injured leg, was batting for Hugh Casey. With first base now empty, Yankee manager Bucky Harris ordered an intentional pass to Reiser, which meant the winning run was on base.

Eddie Stanky was up next. Even though the second baseman was a sharp-eyed batter, the Dodger mastermind, Burt Shotton, pulled a surprise by sending up another right-handed swinger, the veteran Harry ("Cookie") Lavagetto, to replace him. The tactical move worked. Lavagetto banged a double off the right-field wall, scoring the two runners, and not only did Bevens see his no-hit masterpiece demolished, but he also lost the game, 3–2. The pinch two-bagger proved to be Lavagetto's only safety of the Series. The luckless Bevens was left with a dubious entry in the record book: most walks by a pitcher, 10.

Ironically, both Bevens and Lavagetto were making their last major-league appearances in the Series. By the next season, they were both gone, arm trouble cutting short Bevens' career and the years catching up with the long-time Brooklyn infielder.

The 1947 Series is also noted for a magnificent fielding play by an obscure Dodger sub. It occurred in the sixth game, prevented the Yankees from tying the score and helped extend the Series to seven games.

Who was the Dodger fielder who made a magnificent catch in the sixth game of the 1947 Series?

The Dodgers, fighting to stay alive in the Series, had battled in front, 8–5, at Yankee Stadium when the Yankees came to bat in the bottom of the sixth. Joe Hatten was on the mound for Brooklyn. Two Yankees were on base when Joe DiMaggio strode to the plate. He lashed a booming shot deep to left-center. It looked to be a three-run clout. But Al Gionfriddo, now in left field for Brooklyn, sprinted toward the barrier and at the last moment jumped up high into the air and gloved the ball close to the 415-foot marker. The great catch saved the Dodgers' lead and they went on to win, 8–6.

Another amazing catch—and generally conceded to be the greatest in Series annals—was the one made in the opening game of the 1954 Series between the New York Giants and the Cleveland Indians, a series also notable for some unbelievable pinch-hitting heroics by a Giants' bench-warmer. But first, about the catch.

Who was the outfielder who made a great catch during the first game of the 1954 Giants-Indians Series?

Willie Mays was the culprit and he picked a most opportune time, as far as Giant adherents were concerned, to display his legerdemain. The Indians, who had taken the American League pennant with a record number of

111 victories, breaking a five-year Yankee stranglehold on the flag, were favored to beat the Giants. The score was tied, 2–2, as the Indians batted in the top of the eighth in the opener at the Polo Grounds. Sal Maglie was pitching for New York but he was lifted after Larry Doby led off with a walk and Al Rosen singled. Don Liddle relieved and he faced Vic Wertz, who had tripled for Cleveland's two runs in the first and who was to produce a .500 average for the whole Series. Wertz rapped a drive to dead-center that had Mays on the run immediately. Racing with his back to the plate, Willie caught the ball over his shoulder only a few feet away from the 460-foot sign, robbing Cleveland of two runs and Wertz of a triple. It was the closest Cleveland was to come to winning a Series game.

The score remained deadlocked and the game went into the 10th inning, providing the opportunity for a Giants' pinch-hitter to make his Series debut.

Who was the Giants' pinch-hitter who was such a sensation during the 1954 Series?

James Lamar ("Dusty") Rhodes, using his bat like a magic wand, was the hitting sensation of the Series. A fine pinch-batsman during the season, Rhodes, who never won any laurels for his outfielding prowess, outdid himself in the Series. In his first appearance, swinging for Monte Irvin, he came up with Mays and Hank Thompson on base. On the first pitch from Bob Lemon, Dusty smacked a fly to right field that traveled slightly more than 260 feet into the lower stands for what in the Polo Grounds was called a Chinese homer. Chinese or not, a home run it was, and it broke up the game.

Rhodes got into the second game much earlier, manager Leo Durocher sensing he had a smoking bat. Dusty again batted for Irvin in the fifth inning and singled, driving in the Giants' first run. Staying in the game, Rhodes hit a more resounding four-bagger to deep right in the seventh to wrap up a 3–1 Giants triumph.

The Series then moved to Cleveland's Municipal Stadium for the third game, but the Indians' luck and Rhodes' stayed the same. Again Rhodes pinch-hit for Irvin, arriving on the scene in the third with the bases loaded. He ripped a single, bringing in two runs, and the Giants had a 3–0 lead, taking the game at 6–2.

In three pinch-hitting appearances, Rhodes drove in six runs, and knocked in seven in all. He wasn't needed in the fourth and final game as the demoralized Indians went down to defeat, 7–4.

Here are some hot liners (one liners, that is) for you to handle. Did everybody bring his glove?

Who holds the record for playing on the most winning World Series teams?

Lawrence Peter ("Yogi") Berra of the Yankees is the lucky fellow. He has collected the winner's share ten times. He also has played in more Series than anyone else —14 of them.

Who owns the highest batting average for a full Series?

Babe Ruth, who clubbed out ten hits, including three doubles and three homers, in 16 at bats in the 1928 Series for a .625 average as the Yanks swept the St. Louis Cardinals in four games.

Who set the record for the most runs batted in in one World Series?

Bobby Richardson. In the 1960 Series against the Pittsburgh Pirates, the Yankee second baseman came through in the clutch often. He rapped out six singles, two doubles, two triples and a homer and drove in 12 runs—a little better than a-hit-a-run pace. He batted at a .367 clip. Richardson also holds the record for the most hits in one Series, 13, which he set in 1964 against the Cardinals.

Who has scored the most Series runs?

Mickey Mantle, who has crossed the plate 42 times. Mantle also has driven in the most Series runs—40.

Who has the longest hitting streak in Series play?

Hank Bauer hit safely in all seven games of the 1956 and 1957 Series and the first three of the 1958 Series for a streak of 17 games, which was snapped by Warren Spahn in the fourth game. Over that stretch he got 24 safeties and batted .315.

Now it's time to turn to some of the unforgettable pitching triumphs in the World Series—and for a clutch performance there are few to equal the deed of a great veteran in the 1926 Series between the St. Louis Cardinals and the New York Yankees. In the twilight of his career this right-hander capped a brilliant Series in a relief role in the seventh game by thwarting a Yankee threat and nailing down the decision for the Cardinals.

Who was the Cardinal starter who appeared in relief in the last game of the 1926 Series?

Grover Cleveland Alexander, an all-time mound great, who had been winning in the majors since 1911 despite a well-earned reputation as a casual observer of training rules, was the unexpected choice to relieve Jess Haines in that seventh game with the Cards nursing a 3–2 lead starting the seventh inning. Alexander had worked the day before, gaining a 10–2 decision for his second route-going victory of the Series. Not bad for a 39-year-old.

But when the Yankees loaded the bases on Haines with two out, manager Rogers Hornsby beckoned for Alexander. Tony Lazzeri, in his rookie season with the Yankees but already establishing himself as a dangerous hitter, waited at the plate. He swung at the first pitch and missed. He hit the second and lined it down the third-base line foul—but not by much. Alexander wound up and threw the third pitch. Lazzeri swung and missed—a strikeout victim on three pitches.

Alexander was not out of the woods yet. The Yankees still had two more innings to get to the veteran. But he set them down in order in the eighth and after two out in the ninth, he gave up a walk to Babe Ruth. But Ruth made it easy for Alexander by trying to steal second. He was thrown out. Alexander had conquered.

Who pitched the only perfect game in World Series history?

You probably remember that it was Don Larsen who fashioned a masterpiece against the Brooklyn Dodgers in the fifth game of the 1956 World Series. But how well do you remember some of the details? For instance, who was the unlucky pitcher who started for Brooklyn? And who was the final batter and how did the game end?

Sal Maglie started for Brooklyn and he had a perfect game going, too, until the fourth inning. With one out Mickey Mantle smacked a homer. That was all Larsen

needed, but the Yankees got him another run in the seventh and Maglie wound up pitching a five-hitter, normally a winning effort. Larsen, who had been shelled off the mound in the second inning of the second game, was so superb in his control that only one hitter—Pee Wee Reese in the first inning—carried the count to three balls. In all, Larsen threw only 97 pitches!

In the climactic ninth with two out and the 64,519 fans in Yankee Stadium holding their breaths, Dale Mitchell was sent up to pinch hit for Maglie. With the count one ball and two strikes, Mitchell fouled off the next pitch. Then Larsen, using his no-wind-up delivery, threw another fast ball. Mitchell started to swing, stopped—and umpire Babe Pinelli, working behind the plate in a World Series for the last time before retiring, called strike three! Twenty-seven men up, 27 men down. And Larsen had carved out a special niche in World Series history—the only man to pitch a perfect game!

Who holds the most World Series pitching records?

The Yankees' Whitey Ford has set so many World Series records that it's impossible to imagine anyone else taking his place as *the* World Series pitcher. Here are his records: most World Series (11), most World Series games (22), most wins (10), most losses (8), most innings pitched (146), most bases on balls (34), most strikeouts (94), most consecutive scoreless innings pitched (33⅔). As you can see, most of these records are endurance records, for Whitey was a member of the winningest ball club of all time. In fact, there for a while, from the early 1950's to the 1960's, you could no more imagine a Series starting without Whitey Ford than you could imagine one starting without Guy Lombardo playing "The Star-Spangled Banner."

But there is one record that Whitey is especially proud of, and that is the most consecutive scoreless innings pitched. Why? Well, he took it away from another great

World Series pitcher. Who? Why George Herman Ruth, of course, who pitched 29 consecutive scoreless innings in World Series play with the Boston Red Sox.

Ford broke Ruth's record when he shut out the Cincinnati Reds for five innings in the fourth game of the 1961 Series before being forced to retire with a foot injury. At that point he had 32 scoreless innings in a row. The next year against the San Francisco Giants Ford extended the streak to 33⅔ innings in the opening game before he was scored upon. Willie Mays broke the streak in the second inning when he crossed the plate on Jose Pagan's squeeze bunt. Ford went on to win the game, 6–2, and set another record with his 10th Series triumph. It also was Whitey's last winning Series game.

But Babe Ruth still holds a Series pitching record. Do you know what it is?

What is Babe Ruth's only remaining Series pitching record?

Ruth is still the owner of the record for pitching the longest winning Series game—14 innings. He hurled the Boston Red Sox to a 2–1 victory over the Brooklyn Dodgers in the second game of the 1916 Series, doling out six safeties and giving up the only run in the first inning. The next 13 innings were the start of his scoreless-inning streak.

Which pitcher holds the record for most strikeouts in a World Series game?

Just about everybody knows the answer to this one, because it is one of the most sensational, most publicized and, we should add, most deserved records in the books (after all, it was made against the Yankees, who no one can accuse of having World Series jitters).

The Dodgers' Sandy Koufax was the man, and he set the record in the first game of the 1963 Series, striking out 15 Yankees. This record has a personal connotation for me, because I happened to see Carl Erskine strike out 14 Yankees at Ebbets Field to break Howard Ehmke's old record of 13 set in 1929 vs. the Chicago Cubs. The memory of Erskine's feat is based on an association with Susan Hayward, for that day the beautiful movie actress was sitting just a few seats away from me. My attention was really divided: Erskine was throwing that ball as he'd never thrown it before, and Miss Hayward was looking like nothing *I'd* ever seen before. As far as I'm concerned, they don't play ball games like that one anymore.

To get back to Koufax, his niche stands alone. (Does a niche stand alone? Does a niche *stand?*) Remember we said that there was an irony to Maris being the one to break Babe Ruth's home run record. Well, there's no irony with Koufax. From the time he learned to get the ball over the plate, he was supreme. As Tommy Henrich, the Yankees' "Old Reliable," said to me one day: "Check his strikeouts against his bases on balls and you know why Koufax is the best." Henrich and I both agree on that.

6

The Fall Classic Fall Guys

VERNON LOUIS ("Lefty") GOMEZ was not only one of the better lefthanders in Yankee history (he had a won-lost record of 189–102), but he also was one of the wittiest. A famous Gomez quip was the one he made late in his career when his arm had lost some of its zip and he had just struggled through a losing effort: "I'm throwing the ball just as hard as ever but it's not getting to the plate as fast."

For our present purpose, which is to talk about some of the players who are forever remembered because of one critical misdeed in World Series competition, another of Gomez' remarks comes to mind: "I'd rather be lucky than good."

Maybe he was thinking about his Series record. He was in five autumn classics, as the sports writers used to say, and he started seven times. And he was unbeaten! He won six times and was not involved in the decision the seventh. How many pitchers, even the best, the Hall of Famers, can match that? (Answer: None.) Gomez certainly was a good pitcher, but he also had to be lucky.

Now for the unlucky, the losers, the good players who booted one at a vital point and, because the Series is the national institution that it is, had the goat's horns pinned on them permanently.

Let's start with the 1941 Series between the Yankees and the Dodgers. The fourth game. Have you guessed who the "goat" was? Mickey Owen. Here was a guy who was in the majors 13 seasons, who was up there that long not for his bat but for his defensive ability and yet one miscue overshadows his whole career.

What was Mickey Owen's blunder in the 1941 Yankees-Dodgers Series?

The Yankees were leading in the Series, 2 games to 1, but it seemed the Dodgers were on the verge of tying it up on that October 5 afternoon at Ebbets Field. They had taken a 4–3 lead on Pee Wee Reese's two-run homer in the fifth and Hugh Casey, their ace reliever who had come on in the fifth to replace Johnny Allen, was in command of the situation. The Yankees hadn't even put on a strong threat against him. In the ninth Casey got Johnny Sturm to ground out and then he easily handled Red Rolfe's tap back to the mound. Only one out to go!

Tommy Henrich was the batter. The count went to three and two. On the next pitch Henrich swung and missed. The game was over—or was it? The next thing the fans knew Owen was racing to the backstop after the ball. Somehow the pitch had skipped away from the reliable Owen for a passed ball. Now Henrich was on first and Joe

DiMaggio was at bat. DiMaggio singled to left. Casey lost his poise. Charley ("King Kong") Keller came up and whacked the ball off the right field wall for a double. Two runs were in and the Yanks were ahead, 5–4. Bill Dickey walked and Joe Gordon doubled for two more runs and that was the ballgame. The Dodgers were beaten, 7–4, and the Series was just about over.

There are two things that should be said in behalf of Mickey Owen, whose real name was Arnold Malcolm Owen. The first is that Casey is supposed to have thrown an illegal spitball for the third strike, which, if true, helps to explain how the ball got away from Owen. Spitballs are often tough to catch. The other is that Casey rates a share of the blame for the defeat. Owen's passed ball would have been a forgotten incident if the Yankees hadn't crashed through with several hits after it.

Coincidentally, the first prominent "goat" in Series annals was a catcher and, of course, the misplay was a passed ball. It cost the Detroit Tigers a first-game victory over the Chicago Cubs in 1907, and there were also some interesting financial ramifications because of the game's outcome.

Who was the "goat" of the 1907 Tigers-Cubs Series and what was the rhubarb he caused?

Bill Donovan, Detroit's star right-hander who had enjoyed his best season with a 25–4 record, went into the ninth inning of the opener with a 3–1 lead. But the Cubs filled the bases on Frank Chance's single, a hit batsman and third baseman Bill Coughlin's error on Johnny Evers' grounder with one out. One run scored while second baseman Herman Schaefer tossed out Frank Schulte.

Manager Chance then sent Del Howard up to bat for Joe Tinker, who had struck out three times. Donovan threw two strikes past Howard. The Detroit pitcher decided to waste one on the outside. Howard hit at the pitch and struck out. The game should have been over, but Charley Schmidt, the Tigers' catcher, made his contribution to baseball lore by letting the ball get away from him. Steinfeldt dashed home with the tying run on the passed ball.

The Cubs tried to follow up this bit of luck by having Evers steal home moments later. Schmidt foiled the strategy by tagging Evers out. But the damage was done.

The two teams fought through another three innings before darkness forced a halt in the action and the game ended in a 3–3 tie.

The outcome immediately caused a clamor among some of the fans who suspected chicanery. Why were the actions of the players suspect? Because of a decision made just the day before at a meeting of the players' representatives, the club owners and the league officials. Just as it is now, the rule was that the players shared in the receipts of the first four games. One of the players at the meeting asked what would happen if there were a tie game. Would it count as one of the four games or would the players be entitled to the money from the first five games?

The league officials decided that the players would get the additional money from a tie game. And here a tie game had happened the very next day!

The two league presidents, aware of the rumors, discussed how the game had been played, taking note of all the key plays, including Schmidt's passed ball, and how the two teams had argued over every close decision. They declared that the game had been on the "up and up." And so the players shared in the receipts of the first five games, which is as long as the Series went, for the Cubs won the next four. But, to avert any future speculation, the league presidents ruled that thereafter the players' split of the gate would come from only the first four games, however they ended.

Five years later a Giants' outfielder by the name of Fred Snodgrass joined the "bonehead elite" by dropping an easy fly ball that helped the Boston Red Sox win the final game of the 1912 Series, which, incidentally, also had a tie contest—in the second game. While Snodgrass gets all the blame, there are some less remembered crucial plays in that 10th inning.

How did the Giants boot the last game of the 1912 Series with the Red Sox?

The Giants had just taken a 2–1 lead in the top of the 10th on Jack ("Red") Murray's double and Fred Merkle's single. The great Christy Mathewson was pitching for New York. He needed only three outs and the Giants would be world champions. He never got them.

The first Boston batter was Clyde Engle, pinch-hitting for Joe Wood. He lifted an ordinary fly to center but the ball popped out of Snodgrass' glove for a two-base error. Harry Hooper then rapped a long drive that was labeled triple, which would tie the game, but Snodgrass made a tremendous catch to stop Engle from scoring.

After Steve Yerkes walked, Tris Speaker popped up in foul territory between home and first. Chief Meyers, the Giants' catcher, and Merkle, playing first, apparently thought the other would handle it. Neither did—and Speaker had another chance. He belted a single and Engle carried across the tying run.

Mathewson then purposely walked Duffy Lewis, and Larry Gardner, the Boston third baseman, drove a long fly to Josh Devore in right that easily brought in Yerkes with the deciding run and ended the Series.

The luckless Giants, who lost their fourth Series in seven years in 1917, came up with another goat that year. His disgrace was that he chased a runner across home plate.

Who was the Giant player who chased a runner across home plate in the 1917 Series?

The memorable boners, as you may have noticed, almost always occur in final games, which is one reason why they are well remembered, and this one was no exception. The Chicago White Sox had a 3–2 advantage in games when the Series returned to the Polo Grounds on October 15, 1917.

The game was scoreless until the fourth when the Giants' fielders did their pitcher, Rube Benton, wrong. Heinie Zimmerman, whose unhappiest moment was yet to come, started it by throwing wide of first on Eddie Collins' grounder for a two-base error. Dave Robertson, the right fielder, then bobbled Joe Jackson's fly ball for an error. Benton forced Oscar ("Hap") Felsch to hit a bounder to the mound and he threw to Zimmerman at third to catch Collins off the bag.

In the rundown Collins dashed back and forth, stalling for time to permit Jackson to get to third and Felsch to second. Suddenly he noticed that home plate was un-

guarded. So the White Sox second baseman started running home with Zimmerman in futile pursuit. The faster Collins easily won the foot race. The spectacle of the slow-footed Zimmerman chasing Collins across the plate became a permanent Series legend.

Chick Gandil's single brought in Jackson and Felsch, giving the White Sox a 3-0 lead, and the Giants were done. Chicago ended up with a 4–2 victory and John McGraw ended up gnashing his teeth.

But the question before the house is: Why pick on Zimmerman? He did the only thing he could do—chase Collins—since he had no one to throw the ball to. The real culprits were catcher Bill Rariden and first baseman Walt Holke, who should have been backing up the play.

Another "fall" guy was a Cincinnati Reds' catcher, who really was decked in the 1939 Series against the Yankees. He left home plate unprotected, too, although the run that scored while he was described as taking a "snooze" had no effect on the final result. As might be expected, it happened in the final game of that Series.

Who was the Reds' catcher who played the "fall guy" in the 1939 Yankees-Reds Series?

The victim was Ernesto Natali Lombardi, nicknamed "Schnozz," one of the best slugging catchers ever (lifetime batting average: .306). Only the year before he had taken the National League batting crown with a .342 average and had been voted the most valuable player in the league, a fairly rare honor for a member of a non-pennant-winning club. Ernie Lombardi was no threat in the 100-yard dash and he hit more doubles that dwindled into singles because of his lack of speed than he cared to remember. Behind the plate he was a workmanlike receiver.

The Yankee powerhouse, which had racked up the Cubs in four straight in the 1938 Series, was in full momentum against the Reds for the first three games of the 1939 Series and then made it four in a row again, but not without the help of a couple of glaring defensive lapses by the Reds.

In that fourth game at Crosley Field, the Reds had gone ahead, 3–2, with a three-run burst in the seventh inning, chasing Steve Sundra, and then had added a run in the eighth. Their No. 1 pitcher, Bucky Walters, had taken over after Paul Derringer had been lifted for a pinch hitter and Bucky started the ninth with a 4–2 lead. But Yankee "luck," as their foes call it, came to the fore.

After Charley Keller and Joe DiMaggio had singled, Bill Dickey hit a double-play ball to Lonnie Frey, but Billy Myers bobbled the toss at second, Keller scored and all hands were safe. DiMaggio advanced to third on George Selkirk's long fly to right and scored the tying run by beating third baseman Billy Werber's peg home on Joe Gordon's grounder.

Then the roof fell in in the 10th. Frank Crosetti walked, Red Rolfe sacrificed him to second and Myers did it again, mishandling Keller's grass-hopper. One out, Yankees on first and third and DiMaggio up. He lined a single to right and nobody ever got more mileage out of a one-bagger. Here's what happened:

Ival Goodman, the Reds' rightfielder, juggled the ball and finally made a throw to the plate. Crosetti had already scored and Keller was on his way home. He and the ball reached Lombardi at the same time. Keller, a very rugged citizen, barreled into Lombardi and knocked him sprawling and loose from the ball, which rolled a few feet away. DiMaggio, meanwhile, was circling the bases and, seeing the big Reds' catcher stunned on the ground, ran past the inert Lombardi to tally the third run on the play. So the Yankees closed up shop with a 7–4 victory.

Lombardi gets the razz, although King Kong Keller had hit him like the proverbial runaway locomotive, and who remembers that Billy Myers made two damaging errors?

The Series "goats" we've talked about so far have been immortalized for one standout misplay—or have been the victim of a memorable incident—but how about the stars who had to suffer through an entire miserable Series?

Who committed the most errors in Series history?

The unfortunate gentleman was Roger Peckinpaugh, of the Washington Senators, normally a fair fielding short-

stop who was a major-leaguer for 17 seasons. Roger made eight errors in the 1925 Series, and his erratic efforts helped the Pittsburgh Pirates overcome a 3–1 deficit in games and win the Series, the only time until the 1958 Yankees accomplished it that a team was able to surmount such a disadvantage. The ironic thing about Peckinpaugh's disgrace is that he had just been named the most valuable player in the American League.

The Dodgers' Willie Davis has the record for most errors in an inning—three—against the Orioles in 1966.

Who was the Brooklyn Dodger whose failure at bat in the 1952 Series hit a personal all-time low?

Through seven games and 21 official trips to the plate Gil Hodges was engulfed in a slump that left him with an ignominious .000 batting average against the Yankee pitchers. What made his humiliation the harder to bear was that one or two timely base hits in this close Series would have given the Dodgers their first world championship.

Hodges bounced back the next year, though, and belted the ball for a hefty .364 mark, but it didn't help the Dodgers beat the Yanks, who won in six games.

Who holds a record streak for hitting futility in a Series?

Marv Owen, Detroit Tiger third baseman, was the luckless player. Starting with the fifth game of the 1934 Series against the Cardinals, he went hitless 12 straight times. The next year against the Chicago Cubs he didn't get a hit until his last at bat in the sixth and final game, after 19 fruitless attempts, which had made him 0-for-31!

Even the greatest of stars had their off-moments in Series competition.

What famed home-run slugger managed only a paltry .118 average in the 1922 Series?

Yes, it was Babe Ruth who was handcuffed by the Giants. He made up for it the next year by rapping them for a .368 average.

Who was on the mound when the Athletics began their historic 10-run assault in the seventh inning of the fourth game of the 1929 Series?

The man who was working with a big 8–0 lead was the Chicago Cubs' Charley Root when the greatest rally in Series history began. Root was yanked after giving up the first four runs in the epic splurge. Three years later, of course, he was to have another bad moment with Babe Ruth.

The "goat" of that 10-run inning, by the way, was Hack Wilson, Chicago's centerfielder, who lost Mule Haas' liner in the sun. Haas got an inside-the-park homer with two men on that cut the Cubs' lead to 8–7.

And to conclude this chapter on the "losers":

Who holds the Series record for playing on the losing team the most times?

Harold ("Pee Wee") Reese of the Brooklyn Dodgers received the losing player's share six times in seven Series.

7

Founders, Managers and Midgets

Do you know what the toughest question about baseball is?

It's how was the game invented? There's no one answer —because nobody knows for sure!

In 1907 a special committee of officials was named to determine the origin of baseball—who the founder was and where the first game was played. After their investigation they decided Abner Doubleday laid out the first field and organized the first baseball game in Cooperstown, New York, sometime in 1839. And for that reason Cooperstown was selected as the site for the Hall of Fame and Baseball Museum, which were opened in 1939—on the supposed 100th anniversary of baseball.

But that 1907 committee couldn't have been more off base. Later, historians discovered that at the time Doubleday was thought to be inventing baseball in Cooperstown he was a cadet at West Point. Furthermore, there was doubt that he had ever even played the game!

So how did baseball start in our country? The best-informed opinion of the historians is that the sport evolved early in the 1800's from cricket and another English game, rounders, which used posts for bases and had a batter who punched the ball and was put out by being hit with the ball. There were variations of the game known as "Town Ball" and "New York Game."

Some of this confusion about the history of baseball—and the different kinds of baseball—is understandable. What American boy has grown up without playing some variation of baseball? Maybe it was stickball on a city street, where hitting a rubber ball the length of three manhole covers with a broom handle was a homer. Or maybe it was one o'cat (or one old cat) on an empty lot, with four players on a side and one base. Or softball, played with a softer ball than the one in use now, the kind that had an outside stitch. Softball was popular in my time because you didn't need gloves (equipment was scarce in the depression days). When you had gloves, then you played "hard ball," as we called regular baseball. Now there are the well-organized, well-equipped Little Leagues, Babe Ruth Leagues, American Legion Leagues, etc., but I'll bet we had just as much fun in our pick-up games, without uniforms and adult supervision.

But getting back to history. While the name baseball began to be commonly used through the 1820's, 30's and 40's, there was still no standard form of the game until 1846. On this event historians are in complete accord.

Who deserves the credit as the creator of modern baseball?

He was a young surveyor by the name of Alexander Cartwright. A Knickerbocker Baseball Club was formed that year and Cartwright, a member, was given the job of laying out a diamond and devising the rules of play.

Cartwright placed the bases 90 feet apart, set up the foul lines, settled on nine players to a team and three outs to an inning—and even three strikes to a batter! A rule was added that a base runner also could not be put out by throwing the ball at him.

The first game was played at Hoboken, New Jersey, on June 19, 1846, between the Knickerbockers and a team called the New York Nine. Cartwright was the umpire and, ironically, his team was trounced, 23–1!

FOUNDERS, MANAGERS AND MIDGETS

Cartwright's involvement with baseball ended shortly afterward, but he had done his work well. His original contributions to the game were officially recognized when he was elected to the Hall of Fame.

Cartwright laid down the basic principles but it took half a century—until nearly 1900—before baseball was played the way we know it today. Pitchers at first were allowed to throw only underhand (the pitcher's box was 46 feet from home plate then), then side-arm, then shoulder-high and finally, in 1884, overhand. The pitching distance was increased, too, until the present 60 feet 6 inches was established in 1893. And it wasn't until 1887 that a batter no longer could call for a high or low pitch! And at one time nine balls were needed to walk a batter, the number gradually decreasing until the four-ball rule was put in effect in 1889.

In the 1890's the custom of the umpire raising his right arm for a strike started.

Who is given credit for getting the umpires to signal balls and strikes?

Bill ("Dummy") Hoy, an outstanding outfielder who played for St. Louis, Cincinnati and Washington from 1888 to 1902, was a deaf mute. Since he couldn't hear the umpire's call when he was batting, the umpires began the arm gestures to tell him what the count was. And the custom has prevailed.

As any player can tell you, the official scorer is an important man. He's the sole judge on hits and errors— and think how many close plays come up through a season. His decision can mean the difference between a no-hitter and a one-hitter! The scorer's rulings affect batting

123

averages, fielding averages and earned-run averages, and these are the figures on which players negotiate next year's contract. In short, the scorer's decisions can touch a player in his most sensitive area—the pocketbook.

Every fan in the park looks to the scoreboard after one of those borderline hit-or-error cases to see which sign is flashed. But few fans know who the official scorer is and how he is chosen.

FOUNDERS, MANAGERS AND MIDGETS

*How do the American and National Leagues go about
selecting their official scorers and who are they?*

The baseball writers who regularly cover the sport in
each major-league city are the official scorers. Technically
they are appointed by the league president. In practice
each chapter of the Baseball Writers Association of America draws up a list of eligible writers, dividing the number
of home games equally among them. To be eligible, a
writer must have covered at least 100 major-league games
each season for the previous three seasons. This list is sent
to the league office for its approval. After each game, the
official scorer fills out a standard form that includes the
boxscore, other pertinent statistical information and expla-
nations of any involved scoring or other matters under his
jurisdiction, and the form is mailed in to the league office.
The official scorer is paid $30 per game for his services.

A pretty soft touch, you're probably saying to yourself.
But how would you like to be the cause of all those ulcers?
Speaking of ulcers, here are some questions about manag-
ers.

*Who was the youngest man ever to manage a major
league team?*

Lou Boudreau, who was 24 years old when he became
manager of the Cleveland Indians in 1942.

Who managed the most number of years in the majors
is too easy a question. The answer, of course, is Connie
Mack, who directed the fortunes of the Philadelphia Athletics from 1901 to 1950. But the A's weren't the only club
Mack ever managed.

Which team did Connie Mack manage before he went to the Athletics?

While still catching for the Pittsburgh Pirates, Connie Mack became their manager in 1894. He also piloted the club in 1895 and 1896.

How many managers have won ten pennants?

Just two, John McGraw of the New York Giants and Casey Stengel. Stengel became the first manager to win five pennants in a row and then gilded that record by winning the World Series in each of those years (1949 to 1953). But there is another manager who won as many Series as Stengel and has a slightly better Series record.

Which manager has a better Series record than Casey Stengel?

Joe McCarthy of the New York Yankees shares the record with Stengel of having won the most World Series —seven—and was a bit more successful, winning his seven Series titles in nine attempts while Stengel was victorious seven times in ten Series.

Who is the only manager to win pennants in both leagues?

Joe McCarthy again, who piloted the Chicago Cubs to the 1929 pennant before moving over to the Yankees for his successful reign through the 1930's.

FOUNDERS, MANAGERS AND MIDGETS

*Who is the only manager to win World Series with two
different National League clubs?*

Bill McKechnie, who won the 1925 Series with the
Pittsburgh Pirates and the 1940 Series with the Cincinnati
Reds.

*Who is the only manager to win World Series with two
different American League clubs?*

Stanley ("Bucky") Harris, who led the Washington
Senators to the 1924 Series title and 23 years later won the
1947 Series with the New York Yankees.

For you trivia fans, here are a couple of old favorites
that should make you the hit of the party and prove
conclusively that you're over thirty.

*Who was the one-armed outfielder who played with the
St. Louis Browns in 1945?*

Pete Gray, who played in 77 games and batted .218 in
his only season in the majors. He was not the only one-
armed player ever to make the majors. Back in the 1880's
Hugh Daly, who had no left arm, pitched for six seasons—
and even threw a no-hitter! More remarkable, he played
second, short and the outfield in several games.

*Who was the midget who pinch hit for the St. Louis
Browns in 1951?*

His name was Edward Gaedel, and he wore the number ⅛. He was signed by Bill Veeck and used as a pinch

hitter against the Detroit Tigers on August 19, 1951. He walked on four straight pitches thrown by Herb Cain, and small wonder—he was only 43 inches tall.

It was all a publicity stunt, of course, and Veeck may have gotten his idea from James Thurber's classic story "You Could Look It Up," but in Thurber's story the midget's success goes to his head and he begins to think of himself as a slugger, with disastrous results. Read the story, it's one of the best ever written about baseball.

What was Cy Young's full nickname?

Cy Young is the all-time pitching leader: most games (906), most complete games (751), most victories (511) and, naturally, most losses (315). His full name was Denton True Young. When he first started pitching, his fast ball was described as swift as a cyclone. The nickname stuck, but in abbreviated form.

Who was the youngest player ever to appear in a major league game?

Joe Nuxhall, who was only 15 years old when he made his first and only pitching appearance of the season for the Cincinnati Reds in the World War II year of 1944. Seven years went by before Nuxhall next toed a major-league mound!

Here's a question that pops up from time to time because many fans "figure out" the wrong answer.

Who had the higher lifetime batting average, Babe Ruth or Lou Gehrig?

Most people tend to pick Gehrig, thinking of how Ruth was always swinging for the fences, but the Babe still had the higher average: .342 to .340 for Gehrig. This is just another example of how incredible a player Ruth was, and tends to support the oft-heard claim that he was the greatest player in the game. Sometimes I half expect to find out that he held some sort of record even for stolen bases!

There's one record, however, that is Gehrig's own: most consecutive games played.

What is Gehrig's record for most consecutive games?

Gehrig's streak consisted of 2,130 games before his tragic illness forced his retirement early in the 1939 season. Before becoming the regular Yankee first baseman, he was only in 34 games.

Who replaced Gehrig at first for the Yankees?

Ellsworth ("Babe") Dahlgren, who held the job for only two years before he was traded to the Boston Braves in 1941.

What team has lost the most games in a season?

Everybody says the 1962 New York Mets, who went down to defeat 120 times, and they are right—for a 162-game schedule. But the most pathetic team of all was Cleveland of the National League in 1899. In 154 games Cleveland wound up on the short end of the score 134 times! Lo, that poor suffering manager.

Which player was in the majors the longest?

Jimmy ("Mickey") McGuire, who started with Toledo of the American Association in 1884 as a catcher and played for 26 seasons, finishing up with the Detroit Tigers in 1912. He was a non-playing manager in 1909 and 1911.

Which club holds the record for the most consecutive victories?

The New York Giants, who put together a winning streak of 26 games in September, 1916—and they finished in fourth place!

FOUNDERS, MANAGERS AND MIDGETS

Which National League player has won the MVP award two years in a row?

Since the Baseball Writers Association began its annual poll in 1931 to select the most valuable player in each league, only one National Leaguer has been able to win the award for two consecutive years. He was Ernie Banks of the Chicago Cubs, who won in 1958 and 1959.

How many American Leaguers have been voted MVP two years in a row?

Five American Leaguers have been able to win most-valuable-player awards back-to-back. Jimmy Foxx of the Philadelphia Athletics won in 1932 and 1933. Hal Newhouser of the Detroit Tigers was the MVP in 1944 and 1945. Yogi Berra of the New York Yankees captured the award in 1954 and 1955, and he was immediately followed by teammate Mickey Mantle in 1956 and 1957. Roger Maris took the honors in 1960 and 1961.

Which five Hall of Fame members were on the same team?

The Philadelphia Athletics in 1927 and 1928 had Jimmy Foxx, Al Simmons, Lefty Grove, Mickey Cochrane and Ty Cobb on their team.

The rarest fielding play is the unassisted triple play. There has been just one in World Series history, and in the thousands of regular-season games through the years a mere six.

Who made the last unassisted triple play?

Johnny Neun, Detroit Tiger first baseman, made the last one against the Cleveland Indians nearly 40 years ago

—on May 31, 1927. And the last one before that? Why the day before! Jim Cooney, shortstop for the Chicago Cubs, made all three putouts against the Pittsburgh Pirates on May 30, 1927. It's either a feast or a famine.

By the way, the lone Series unassisted triple play was made by Billy Wambsganss (yes, that's how it's spelled), a second baseman for the Cleveland Indians who turned the trick against the Dodgers in 1920.

I'm going to close this chapter and this whole section on baseball with what I'll call a CHALLENGE ROUND SPECIAL. It's a question about a situation the likes of which make baseball endlessly fascinating:

In the last game of the season the Brooklyn Dodgers were only a few feet away from tying the Philadelphia Phils for the 1950 pennant—the few feet representing the distance from home plate when Cal Abrams was thrown out. He was trying to score in the last half of the ninth of a 1–1 game the Phils went on to win in the 10th, 4–1.

Who was the outfielder who threw out Abrams and who got the hit that Abrams tried to score on?

Richie Ashburn, the Phils centerfielder, cut down Abrams at home after Duke Snider had singled. The play saved the game and the pennant for the Phils, but what's fascinating is that it never should have happened.

Ordinarily any runner will score from second on a hit to center, especially when there are two outs, and Abrams was faster than most runners. Also Ashburn did not own one of the stronger throwing arms among National League outfielders.

So how did it happen that Abrams was thrown out? Because of a "broken" play—to use the football term—meaning that someone missed a signal. With Snider at bat, the Phils gave the sign for a pickoff play at second. Granny Hamner, the shortstop, moved over to take the throw and Ashburn moved in to back up the play. The only thing wrong was that Robin Roberts had missed the pickoff sign! He pitched to the plate, Snider singled and Abrams was off and running. Except that Ashburn was now in shallow centerfield and it was simple for him to throw in to Andy Seminick, the catcher, and nail Abrams.

...WHAT KEPT YA?

8

Diamonds in the Ring

CASSIUS CLAY (or Muhammad Ali, as he prefers to be called) is the most controversial figure in the fight world today—perhaps in all of sports, for that matter. Like him or not, you cannot ignore him, and it looks as though he's going to be around for quite a while. As Clay himself puts it: "Somewhere there's a twelve-year-old kid who's going to beat me," and it may be that Clay is right; a whole new generation of boxers will have to come along before there is anyone who can match him.

With all the publicity Clay has received, two central facts have often been overlooked by both sports writers and fans. First, Clay is probably the fastest heavyweight ever to step into a ring, and second, he is a very big man (6'3", 208 lbs.).

For some reason, people seldom think of Clay as a big man. Perhaps this is because their image of a heavyweight was set by fighters like the great Rocky Marciano, squat, solid men who stood there like rocks of granite or relentlessly stalked their opponents. Clay is another type of fighter altogether. He moves constantly, seldom engages in slugging contests, and when he does score a knockout, usually does it so fast that some observers have actually doubted that any punch was landed.

All I can say about Clay is that he fights his own style, and as long as it's successful there is no reason in the world for him to change it. Actually, Clay is closer to the modern image of the big athlete than any other heavyweight. It wasn't so long ago we thought of pro football players as just so many behemoths, but now we expect 250-pound linemen to run like sprinters. Why shouldn't we expect the same of our heavyweights?

The most controversial fight of Clay's career so far was his rematch with Sonny Liston for the championship at Lewiston, Maine, on May 25, 1965. Clay knocked Liston out in what may have been the shortest championship bout on record—except no one seems to know just when the bout ended.

With millions of witnesses listening on radio and watching on television, the time of the end of the bout was interpreted in a number of ways. Those who witnessed the fight via the communications media timed the knockout at one minute 42 seconds, but Maine boxing officials said the end came at one minute. However, the bout which slipped from the control of the referee—Jersey Joe Walcott, a fair-minded former champion—was not declared over until two minutes 17 seconds had gone by. The two fighters actually squared off to resume trading blows. Later reports also created more lore for "long count" fans, with one noted expert, who sat beside the timekeeper, testifying that Walcott had motioned for the timekeeper to stop the clock in order to wave Clay to a neutral corner and then resumed the count, which came to 20 in all.

To compound the confusion Clay was credited with knocking out Liston with one short right-hand punch—a phantom punch that many members of the press reporting the fight and virtually all others swore they hadn't seen.

What was the shortest title fight on record?

Since the Clay-Liston fight has been ruled out, the record book shows that on April 6, 1914, Al McCoy stopped George Chip in 45 seconds in Brooklyn, N. Y., to win the world middleweight title. In a nontitle bout, Mike DeJohn took only 47 seconds to dispose of Charley Powell on November 6, 1959, at Syracuse, N. Y.

The fighter to take the fastest express to his dressing room in a heavyweight title bout was Irish Jem Roche who got his ticket from Tommy Burns, the champion, on St. Patrick's Day, March 17, 1908, and, of course, the bout was held on Irish soil. Burns swarmed all over Roche in a Dublin ring and before many onlookers were aware of what was happening Roche was on his way out. The end came at 1:28—the shortest heavyweight title fight on record.

The sport of boxing has no doubt provoked as many bar-room and living-room arguments as there have been fights in the prize ring. Someone is always leading with his chin to put the record straight. The rest of this chapter deals with some of those questions that inspire chin-leading.

Like most fans you probably associate the words "long count" with the second Jack Dempsey-Gene Tunney heavyweight title fight in Chicago on September 22, 1927. Undoubtedly it was boxing's most famous and most important long count, but there have been several other bouts in which the timekeepers and the referees were unable to synchronize their basic arithmetic.

What was the longest count in a fight?

When Dempsey decked Tunney and then failed to go to a neutral corner, a tactic that proved costly for Dempsey, the knockdown was timed at 14 seconds by some experts and at 16 by others. Whatever the elapsed time, it afforded no knockout for Dempsey who lost the decision and his chance to regain the title Tunney had taken from him a year and a day earlier.

But twice that length of time was consumed for a long count on March 12, 1948, at Madison Square Garden in a bout between the great French middleweight, Marcel Cerdan, and Lavern Roach, a good journeyman battler. Cerdan had tagged Roach with a hard blow that sent him falling to the canvas in the second round, but moments later Cerdan, reeling from the impact of his own punch, went sprawling to the canvas himself. Roars from the fans filled the Garden and confusion filled the minds of the officials.

Cerdan was up in a flash, and while the timekeeper, Jack Watson, and the referee, Arthur Donovan, vehemently argued whether Roach was officially knocked down, time marched on. The length of the knockdown was reported to be 32 seconds—enough time for Cerdan to have knocked out Roach three times. The Frenchman finally won on a kayo in the eighth round.

The "long count" when skillfully manipulated by either official or unofficial "hanky-panky" served as a reprieve for a fighter facing imminent annihilation. While no official time for the knockdown of Kid McCoy by Kid Carter in the second round of their bout on May 19, 1902, at

Philadelphia, is known, it was reported that it occurred "before two minutes of the round had been fought," with the bell saving McCoy. The timekeeper for that bout must have been counting the house.

The heavyweights are the glamour boys of boxing. They get the biggest purses and the most publicity, but the road to success is not strewn with lilies. Most of them have tasted bitter defeat.

How many heavyweight champions retired undefeated?

Technically only four—James J. Jeffries, Gene Tunney, Joe Louis and Rocky Marciano. However, Jeffries and Louis returned to ring combat after they gave up their crowns, trying to make comebacks at which they were unsuccessful. Tunney and Marciano, on the other hand, never laced the gloves again after they hung them up.

Jeffries, a popular champion, held the title for six years, taking on all comers and disposing of them easily before retiring in March 1905. He was forced into a comeback by a hero-worshipping public and he climbed through the ropes again in 1910, trying unsuccessfully to wrest the title from ageless Jack Johnson, boxing's first Negro heavyweight champion.

Tunney retired after his second defense against Tom Heeney on July 26, 1928. His first defense was against Dempsey, from whom he had won the title. Joe Louis relinquished the crown on March 1, 1949, after 25 defenses, the most by any heavyweight champion, but he returned to fight many exhibition bouts and also tried unsuccessfully to regain the title from Ezzard Charles in 1950. Marciano, after six defenses, announced his farewell to the sport on April 27, 1956.

In the lighter divisions it has not been uncommon for former champions to regain their titles, but among heavyweights the feat is a rarity.

How many former heavyweight champions have regained the title?

Only one. Floyd Patterson became the first man to take back the heavyweight crown on June 20, 1960, when he knocked out Ingemar Johansson of Sweden in the fifth round at the Polo Grounds in New York. Patterson was 25 years old when he achieved the feat that evaded greater champions than he. The year before he had lost the title to Johansson on June 26 in a see-saw donnybrook in which Floyd was floored seven times before he gave up the ghost of consciousness in the third round. But Patterson established his clear-cut superiority over the Hammer of Thor on March 13, 1961, at Miami Beach, despite having been floored three times himself during the bout.

No former light-heavyweight champion has ever regained the title.

Some great fighters have never been champions. Some have held two different titles and many have fought in different divisions.

Who was the only fighter to hold three world titles simultaneously?

Remember Henry ("Hammerin' Hank") Armstrong? The fighter who was also called "Perpetual Motion" won the featherweight title on October 29, 1937, with a knockout over Petey Sarron. Less than a year later, on May 31, 1938, he took the welterweight crown from Barney Ross on a decision and that same year, on August 17, he gained a decision over Lou Ambers and took the lightweight diadem. Later in life Armstrong became a minister.

The knockout, like the home run in baseball, is the most dramatic and convincing way to display supremacy, and the one-round knockout, like a bases-loaded homer, is even more so, leaving its victims dumbfounded, hurt and beaten.

Which fighter scored the most one-round knockouts?

While the record book itself seems incapable of encompassing this kind of record, the fact that Jack Dempsey scored more than 60 one-round kayos, including exhibition bouts, establishes at least a gauge.

Dempsey racked up 23 one-round kayos before he became champion and even suffered a setback in the opening round at the hands of Jim Flynn in 1917. A year later, Dempsey atoned for that one by doing the same to Flynn. Dempsey, however, never scored a one-round knockout in a defense of his title, although no fighter could have come as close to doing it as he did in his brawl with Luis Firpo in New York on September 14, 1923.

Which fighter scored the most one-round knockouts in title bouts?

Joe Louis was the most destructive exponent of the one-round knockout in title bouts. He acquired the technique in his first pro fight, July 4, 1934, when he prostrated Jack Kracken at Chicago (Louis's part of the purse was $52). Louis scored ten one-round knockouts in his 71-fight pro career, and as champion he did it an astounding five times. His quickest and most brutal one was inflicted in two minutes and four seconds the night he used his own self-styled blitzkrieg on Max Schmeling, an emissary out of Hitler's Germany who got a telegram from the Führer before the fight exhorting him to uphold the honor of the Master Race.

The confusion that often accompanies a fight when officials are at odds interpreting the rules brings us to another important facet of the sport.

How are fights scored?

In different parts of the United States there are several ways of scoring a bout. In New York State, the referee and the judges score the fight on both a round-by-round and a point system. If a bout ends in a draw on the basis of rounds, then the officials revert to their point scores to determine a winner. The point system ranges from 1 to 4. A fighter's display of basic tactics is taken into account, and if he wins a round by a slim margin he gets a point, the loser zero; a decisive round will earn 2 points; a one-sided round or one in which a knockdown has been scored will earn 3 points, and a one-sided round with two or more knockdowns, 4 points.

In most states affiliated with the National Boxing Association the 5-point must system is the rule. That is, a fighter winning a round, even if only by a shade, will get 5 points. A knockdown and a clear superiority in a round will give the winner a 5 to 3 margin, and so forth. In a similar way a 10-point must system is used in Massachusetts, Ohio, Texas and Miami Beach.

New Jersey uses a rounds system (no points). In California a 5-point system is in effect, but the winner can receive anywhere from 1 to 5 points, the loser zero. It's not uncommon for a round to be scored 0–0.

As you can see, there's a lot to be said for the knockout. It does away with all that arithmetic, it settles the issue once and for all, and there is something infinitely satisfying in seeing someone twice as big as you stretched out on the canvas. There was one fighter who seldom disappointed the fans on this score.

Which fighter holds the record for most knockouts?

Dapper, mustachioed Archie Moore, who had 226 bouts and won more than half of them—138—by knockouts. Moore started his career in 1936, but not until late in his career, in 1952, did he get a crack at a title, beating Joey Maxim for the light-heavyweight crown. He fought Rocky Marciano for the heavyweight title in 1955 and was knocked out in the ninth round. He retired in 1964.

A knockdown, while not always a prelude to a knockout, is a good measure of how soon a knockout might occur. Many fights have had many knockdowns, and in one real donnybrook, with both fighters hitting the canvas frequently, it was not the outcome that was in doubt, but which fighter would score a knockout first.

What is the record for most knockdowns in a fight?

Would you believe 49? It's hard to imagine two men having the stamina to last through so many knockdowns, but Battling Nelson, the great Danish lightweight champion, floored Christy Williams 42 times and hit the deck seven times himself before he put Williams away in the 17th round in a nontitle bout on December 26, 1902.

Williams shares the record for most knockdowns suffered by one fighter with Jack Havlin, who did the bouncing act over 29 rounds against Tommy Warren in San Francisco on September 25, 1888, when men were men. Warren never dirtied his trunks.

What was the longest glove fight on record?

Can you imagine two men belting each other for 110 rounds, a total of seven hours and 19 minutes, and nobody winning? That's what the two "gentlemen" Andy Bowen and Jack Burke did on April 6, 1893, at New Orleans. The fight was called a draw by the referee when neither man could continue.

What is the record for most knockdowns in one round?

The answer to this one brings us back to the Dempsey-Firpo fight, considered by many experts to have been the fiercest battle ever fought. It lasted only two rounds, with Dempsey crushing the Wild Bull of the Pampas to the canvas seven times in the first three minutes. During those 180 seconds, Dempsey came within a whisker of losing his title when he was knocked out of the ring while a crowd of 90,000 at the Polo Grounds went into a wild uproar. In all, there were nine knockdowns in the first round. Firpo went down three more times in the second round as Dempsey, springing to the attack the instant the courageous Argentine rose, pummeled him savagely.

Here are some fast questions and answers to challenge you.

What was the largest live gate in boxing history?

The second Dempsey-Tunney fight at Soldiers Field, Chicago. The gate was $2,658,660! And remember, there was no TV money in those days!

What was the largest live attendance at a fight?

The first Dempsey-Tunney fight at Sesqui-Centennial Stadium, Philadelphia, September 23, 1926. The attendance was 120,757. On August 18, 1941, Tony Zale and Billy Pryor fought before 135,132 in Milwaukee, at the Fraternal Order of Eagles Free Show.

How many fighters have never been defeated in a pro career?

Four. Rocky Marciano (1947–1955), 49 fights; Jack McAuliffe (1884–1897), 53 bouts; Larry Foley (1866–1888), 22 fights; Jimmy Barry (1891–1899), 70 bouts.

Who refereed the most title bouts?

Yes, referees set records too. Arthur Donovan refereed 14 title fights.

Who was youngest fighter to win a heavyweight title?

Floyd Patterson, at 21, was the youngest fighter to win a heavyweight title. Two other youngsters who did it were Cassius Clay (22) and Joe Louis (23). Jersey Joe Walcott was the oldest, at 37.

There is one aspect of the sport of boxing that has always fascinated me, but I think I'll save it for a new chapter.

9

The Hungry Gladiators

BACK in the first chapter I asked myself the question, "What makes a good fighter?" The answer I gave myself then was "poverty," but it might just as well have been "nationality." For the truth is that the history of any nationality or ethnic group in this country is marked by extreme poverty in its earliest years. And one of the traditional ways for a nationality group to gain some measure of respect and economic betterment in this country is through sports—particularly boxing. One can almost read the fortunes of nationality groups by their progressive involvement in and then gradual withdrawal from the sports scene. When one group no longer identifies with a boxer but with a businessman or a professional man or a politician, then that group has taken the first step away from poverty, prejudice, and parochialism and has entered the main stream of American life. But what a legacy they leave to the sports world! The classic case in point is that of the Irish. They came

to this country to escape famine and the worst living conditions of just about any place on earth. Here they were given the most menial jobs available; they were poor, they were abused, and they were hated, but they weren't starving, and to an Irishman then that was just about everything. At first they were probably ashamed of what they were, but gradually they began to realize that they could lay more track, carry more hod, dig more canals—and yes, fight more rounds and knock out more opponents—than anybody else. Their first hero, the first man they could all identify with and be proud of, was John L. Sullivan. This sense of identity and pride was a tremendous step upward for the Irish, and it wasn't long before their natural gift for politics (the legacy of hundreds of years of dealing with absentee landlords, military governors, occupation troops and the like) came to the surface and they made the next step out of the ghetto and onto the stage of local, state and, finally, national politics. But that first step had to be taken before the second, and it is not an exaggeration to say that it would not have been possible without an ethnic hero like John L. Sullivan.

Of course, there will always be Irish fighters (who could imagine—or want—a card without a Battling Murphy or Killer Kelly on it?), but my point is that an Irishman doesn't *have* to fight anymore to gain respect and recognition. And anyway it's easier for him to become a lawyer.

The Irish haven't dominated the sport of boxing for years, but other nationality groups have, according to their position in the socio-economic scale, and they too have gone their ways, just as the Irish have. So lets investigate a few of these fighters by their national origins, remembering that they not only did great service to the sport of boxing but also to their national or ethnic group and, ultimately, to their country.

The following aren't so much questions as excuses for me to talk about some of my favorites. And incidentally, these are the sort of questions I like to be challenged with. Sure there are facts and statistics and dates involved, but more important, these are real people who had something going for them that you and I have no idea about. It's only fitting that we should begin with the Irish.

Who were five great fighters of Irish descent?

Here are my choices. It so happens that all five were world champions, if not necessarily among the greatest in their divisions; in the other nationality groups I've selected a few who because of circumstances never won a world title.

What better name to start with than the mighty John L. Sullivan, the Boston Strong Boy? The last and acknowledged as the greatest of the bare-knuckle champions, he was the first national boxing hero. After he gained the heavyweight title in 1882 by knocking out Paddy Ryan in the ninth round in Mississippi City, Miss., he toured the country, taking on all challengers in regular bouts and exhibitions. In those days the sport was illegal or sub rosa

in many areas. John L. fought wherever he could, on barges, in back rooms of saloons, in theaters. He won the acclaim and affection of fans from coast to coast as he made good on his boast: "I can lick any man in the world!" And he never did lose so long as they fought with their bare fists. One of the all-time unforgettable fights was his marathon battle with Jake Kilrain on July 8, 1889, in Richburg, Miss., with a sidebet of $10,000. The two matched punches for nearly two and a half hours before Sullivan decked Kilrain for good in the 75th round! A fitting end to an era, for it was the last bare-knuckle championship bout.

So great was John L.'s popularity that he recorded another first the following year by becoming the first boxer to star on Broadway, playing the leading role in a melodrama entitled "Honest Hearts and Willing Hands." Looking for new worlds to conquer, he traveled to Europe and England, putting his pugilistic skills on display before appreciative audiences that included the Prince of Wales. Now an international celebrity, Sullivan returned to America and was able to say: "Shake the hand that shook the hand of the Prince of Wales." Soon his admirers changed the saying to "Shake the hand that shook the hand of John L. Sullivan."

It was said that "strong men wept" at the news of the end of John L.'s reign in 1892. James J. ("Gentleman Jim") Corbett, a superlative boxer, proved too quick and nimble with his fists and feet and brought down the aging idol in 21 rounds in New Orleans.

And then there is Mickey Walker, the Toy Bulldog from Elizabeth, New Jersey. He was aptly nicknamed; none had a greater fighting heart. A welterweight and middleweight champion, he showed his pugnaciousness and courage by taking on light-heavyweights and heavy-weights. What did it matter to him that he had to give away 30 and 40 and 50 pounds in weight? About the only fight he couldn't get into was World War I. He was turned down for being too small! He earned his first title—welterweight—when he defeated Jack Britton in 15 rounds in the Garden on November 1, 1922. He lost the crown to Pete Latzo four years later but came back to win the middleweight championship from Tiger Flowers in Chicago on December 3, 1926. And he gave that title up to battle the big boys! He had memorable contests with such top-notchers as Tommy Loughran, Jack Sharkey, Maxie Rosenbloom and Max Schmeling.

Gene Tunney, the first to retire as undefeated heavy-weight champion, was born in New York City on May 25, 1898. He started boxing as a pro in 1915 and gained his first fame after enlisting as a Marine during World War I. In 1919 in France he won the American Expeditionary Force light-heavyweight title after a series of eliminations and then defeated the A.E.F. heavyweight champion, Bob Martin, in a special four-round bout. He resumed fighting in America later that year. An excellent boxer with a powerful punch, Tunney made his way up through the light-heavyweight ranks and took the American title with a 12-round decision over Battling Levinsky on January 13, 1922. On May 23, 1922, he was handed his only defeat in the ring by the fabulous Harry Greb, dropping the decision in a bruising 15-rounder. He came back to regain the title from Greb on February 23, 1923, and beat Greb again later the same year. He gave up the light-heavyweight title to enter the heavyweight ranks. By the end of 1925 he was established as the No. 1 contender to Jack Dempsey and they met on September 23, 1926, in

Philadelphia, with Tunney outpointing the Manassa Mauler in ten rounds to become the heavyweight king. They were rematched the following September 22 in Chicago in the famous "bout of the long count." Tunney, always a cool and intelligent craftsman who knew what he was doing every second in the ring, used the extra respite given him when he was floored and Dempsey failed to go to a neutral corner, to box his way out of trouble and go on to get the 10-round decision. The bout is also remem-

bered for the record purse Tunney received—$990,000—the highest paid to a fighter up to that time. After knocking out Tom Heeney on July 26, 1928, Tunney retired and entered the business world, becoming an important executive in several companies. His ring record shows only one blemish—the loss to Greb—and he knocked out more than half of his opponents—41 in 76 bouts!

Next, how about an Irish-American fighter who was actually born in Ireland—Belfast, to be exact. Jimmy ("Baby Face") McLarnin, one of the finest ringmen and a champion in a golden era for welterweights. Despite his boyish countenance, he was a rugged battler and he suffered only one knockout, by Ray Miller in Detroit on November 30, 1928, in a 13-year career and 77 bouts, of which he won 63. He captured the title by belting out Young Corbett in the first round in Los Angeles on May 29, 1933. Then followed three bruising 15-rounders with Barney Ross in which he lost, regained, and then lost the crown again. He stopped Benny Leonard's comeback bid with a sixth-round KO and split two decisions with Tony Canzoneri and defeated Lou Amberg before hanging up his gloves in 1936.

My fifth Irish favorite is Philadelphia Jack O'Brien, who was born in Philadelphia, naturally. He was a classy light-heavyweight, just about the best ever. He started as a pro in 1896 and took the title when he floored Bob Fitzsimmons in the 13th at San Francisco on December 20, 1905. Twice he challenged Tommy Burns, the heavyweight champion, getting a draw and then losing by decision in two 20-round slugfests. He retired in 1912 after 181 bouts, losing only seven!

That makes five, but there are two others I'd like to mention.

THE HUNGRY GLADIATORS

Terry McGovern, one of the all-time great bantam and featherweights, was born in Johnstown, Pennsylvania, on March 9, 1880. He ran up a winning streak of 19 after he began fighting as a pro in 1897. After the streak was interrupted by Tim Callahan, whom he lost to on a foul on July 23, 1898, McGovern embarked on another streak that went on for three years and included 45 matches, most of them won with knockouts. In the process he won the bantamweight crown with a one-round kayo of Pedlar Palmer at Tuckahoe, New York, on September 12, 1899. After he vacated the title at the end of the year, he stepped up to the featherweights and dethroned George Dixon, stopping him in eight, on January 9, 1900. Young Corbett ended McGovern's reign and victory streak on November 28, 1901, with a second-round KO at Hartford. He fought until 1908 and finished with the impressive total of 34 knockout victims in 77 bouts; he lost just four.

And then there is James J. Braddock, the "Cinderella" man. You've got to admire the Jersey City longshoreman who went from the depression relief rolls one year to the heavyweight championship the next. He started his climb by knocking out a bright young prospect named Corn Griffith in a preliminary to the Max Baer-Primo Carnera title bout. Twelve months and two victories later he got his shot at boxing's biggest prize. A 20–1 underdog against Baer, who packed a fierce wallop in his right hand, Braddock tucked his chin under his left arm and coolly outboxed Baer for 15 rounds in the Long Island City Bowl to produce one of the ring's most tremendous upsets on the night of June 13, 1935.

Yet, perhaps I respect Braddock even more for the way he lost his title. Joe Louis was at his magnificent best in their Chicago match on June 22, 1937. The Irishman was absorbing a fearful beating. His manager, Joe Gould, wanted to throw in the towel. But the battered and bleeding Braddock growled: "No, I won't lose my title sitting on a stool. [Take note, Sonny Liston] He'll have to knock me out." And Braddock went out like a champion in the eighth round.

Who were five great fighters of Polish or Slavic descent?

Considering that only about one-fifth as many immigrants came to America from the Slavic areas as from Ireland and Italy, it's remarkable that the excellence of their fighters is equal to the others.

No. 1 in everybody's book has to be Stanley Ketchel (Stanislaus Kiecal), rated the greatest middleweight in history despite the tragic shortening of his career when he was shot to death by a farmer at the age of 24. He was nicknamed the Michigan Assassin because of his pulverizing fists that demolished 46 foes by the KO route in 61 bouts! He began in the ring in 1903 at 17 and in four years was the champion, disposing of Joe Thomas in 32 rounds. Despite a weight handicap, in 1909 he even floored the great Jack Johnson in a heavyweight title bout before being knocked out himself. He lost his middleweight crown to Billy Papke in 12 rounds after he was "suckered" at the opening bell. Ketchel came out to shake hands and instead Papke rocked him with a right that dazed him for the rest of the bout. Ketchel got his revenge in the return match, pounding Papke into submission in 11 rounds at San Francisco on November 26, 1908, and becoming the first middleweight king to regain his title.

Another great middleweight was Tony Zale (Anthony Florian Zaleski) who came out of the steel mills of Gary,

Indiana, as tough as metal. He had a potent KO punch, too; he put away 46 opponents in 88 bouts. Classic swinging-from-the-floor bouts were his three title matches with another belter, Rocky Graziano, all three of which ended in knockouts! Zale finished Rocky in the sixth round of their first meeting to keep the middleweight crown on September 27, 1946, was knocked out in the same round in the rematch nine months later, and then floored Rocky in the third brawl in round No. 3 in Newark on June 10, 1948. Zale ended his ring days three months later when he dropped the title on a 12-round KO to Marcel Cerdan, the Frenchman.

Then there was Gus Lesnevich (Russian), light-heavyweight champion who fought from 1934 to 1949. He beat Anton Christoforidis in 15 rounds for the National Boxing Association Title on May 22, 1941, and then made himself undisputed boss of the 175-pound class by outpointing Tami Mauriello on November 14 of the same year. After World War II service in the Coast Guard, Gus successfully defended his title by knocking out Freddie Mills in London in the 10th round in 1946, and by twice decking Billy Fox, the second time in less than a round, in 1948. He then lost the crown to Mills on a 15-round decision in London on July 26, 1948.

Another was Pete Latzo (Slovak), welterweight champion out of the coal-mining regions of Pennsylvania. He began boxing at 17 in 1919 and punched his way up through the 147-pound ranks until he wrested the title from Mickey Walker in Scranton on a 10-round decision on May 20, 1926. After he was dethroned by Joe Dundee in 15 rounds the next year, Latzo moved up to the middleweights and even battled the light-heavies. He twice challenged Tommy Loughran, the light-heavy titleholder in

159

1928, losing both times by decisions. He hung up his gloves in 1934 after 150 bouts; he was knocked out only twice.

Finally there is Fritzie Zivic of the Fighting Zivics of Pittsburgh (Croatian), welterweight champion. The fifth and last brother to enter the ring (Jack, Pete, Joe and Eddie preceded him), Fritzie was a busy and durable campaigner with 230 bouts over 18 years. No respecter of Marquis of Queensberry rules, he was a rough and tough battler. After one particularly savage bout, Fritzie had head X-rays taken and was told by the doctor that he had the hardest head the medic had ever seen! He reigned as welter champ after defeating Henry Armstrong on October 4, 1940, and then kayoed Armstrong in a return match three months later.

Who were five great Jewish fighters?

Heading the list is Benny Leonard, a lightweight champion whom many consider the greatest ever, and one of only two 135-pound kings to retire undefeated. A boxing master par excellence, he often went through an entire fight without getting his carefully slicked-down hair mussed. From 1917 to 1924 he dominated his division and also fought leading welterweights. He then stayed out of the ring for six years before making a comeback as a welterweight in 1931 and 1932. He had 209 bouts in all, winning 68 by knockout, and was the loser in only five.

Barney Ross (Barnet Rosofsky), was another top lightweight and welterweight champion in the 1930's when there were so many outstanding fighters. After taking the lightweight title from Tony Canzoneri in New York on September 12, 1933, he gave it up and struck for the

THE HUNGRY GLADIATORS

unior welter crown, beating Sammy Fuller only two months later. By 1934 he and Jimmy McLarnin had the first of three slambang 15-rounders for the welterweight title, with Ross winning the first and the third. He held the title until Henry Armstrong defeated him on May 31, 1938, his last bout. In 82 matches he was never knocked out and lost only four by decision.

Then there was the unforgettable Maxie Rosenbloom, a light-heavyweight champion who belied his nickname of Slapsy Maxie by his astute portrayals of comic characters on the screen after his boxing days were over. His later fame in the movies tends to obscure what a fine ringman he was. From 1923 to 1939 he engaged in 289 bouts with light-heavy and heavyweights and was knocked out only twice! He gained the light-heavy crown on July 14, 1932 from Lou Scozza in Buffalo and wore it for two years unti a 15-round loss to Bob Olin.

Fourth is Louis ("Kid") Kaplan, a featherweight champion who was born in Russia. His family emigrated to American when he was five years old. A tremendous boxer, he ranks among the all-time greats. After four year as a pro, he took the title by belting out Danny Kramer in the ninth round on January 2, 1925. He defeated the best of his class until he had to give up the crown in 1927 when he was unable to make the weight. He continued as a lightweight until 1933 and had 131 bouts in all.

Lew Tendler, who will be forever known as "the man who was talked out of a world championship," was born in Philadelphia on September 28, 1898. He started as a bantamweight at the age of 15 and then fought as a featherweight, lightweight and welterweight. But he made his reputation as one of the sport's hardest-punching lightweights. He didn't suffer a loss in the ring until 1919, although his record is dotted with many no-decision matches. By 1923 he got his shot at the world lightweight title held by the great Benny Leonard. He had the "dancing master" in trouble in a late round when he slowed his attack because of Leonard's "chatter," which gave Leonard time to box out of danger and retain his crown with a 15-round decision. The next year Tendler moved up to the welterweight class and challenged Mickey Walker for the title, dropping a 10-rounder on June 2 in Philadelphia. He fought for five more years and retired in 1928 after 168 bouts, 37 knockouts and 11 defeats. As so many fighters have done, Tendler entered the restaurant business, in

THE HUNGRY GLADIATORS

Philadelphia and Atlantic City, and, unlike most, he was as successful out of the ring as in.

That makes five, but there are a few more I'd like to bring up because people don't realize the tremendous contribution that Jews have made to the fight game—and as *fighters*, not as promoters and managers.

Abe Attell, one of the all-time standout featherweight champions, was born in San Francisco on February 22, 1884. He was 16 years old when he began fighting for money in 1900. And what a start he did make! He compiled one of the more lustrous winning streaks among pro debuts, showing knockout power that was extremely rare for the 126-pound division. In his first year he put away 15 of his first 16 opponents—only one bout ending in a decision—and none of the kayos came later than the fourth round! He won his first 32 bouts before the streak was snapped by a draw with George Dixon a little more than 12 months after he had turned professional. Two months later—October 28, 1901—he fought Dixon again for the vacant featherweight title and took a 15-round decision. For the next 11 years he was supreme among the 126-pounders, defeating challengers for his title 12 times! Johnny Kilbane finally made Attell step down from the throne on February 22, 1912, at Vernon, California, in a blistering 20-rounder. Abe retired at the end of 1913 except for one comeback fight in 1917 when he was knocked out. In his record of 168 bouts, he KO'd 47 foes and was the loser only ten times.

Ted ("Kid") Lewis, who was born Gershon Mendeloff in London, England, on October 24, 1894, was world welterweight king twice and held the Lord Lonsdale belt as the welter and middleweight champ in Britain. He started as a bantamweight in 1910 and before he quit the ring for good in 1929 had battled his way through the ranks to where he was taking on light-heavyweights and heavyweights.

His first title was the British featherweight crown, which he won by stopping Alec Lambert in London in the 17th round on October 6, 1913. After winning the European featherweight title from Paul Til in London on a foul in the 12th round on February 2, 1914, Lewis traveled to Australia for several bouts before coming to America. Three months after his arrival, Lewis had his first match with Jack Britton on March 26, 1915—a 10-round no-decision affair—and it marked the beginning of one of the historic series in boxing. He and Britton met 20 times, often with the world welterweight title as the prize. The final tally showed three victories for Lewis, four for Britton, one draw and 12 no decisions. From the time Lewis beat Britton for the title in 12 rounds in Boston on August 31, 1915, they had a two-man monopoly of the crown for the next six years. After losing the title to Britton the following April, Lewis regained it two months later and wore the crown for two years before Britton took it over again on March 17, 1919. His last meeting with Britton was a 15-round loss in early 1921. Shortly afterward he returned to England and boxed there and in Europe with success through the rest of the 1920's. It was estimated he had more than 400 fights but the *Ring Record Book* lists only 250, of which he won 65 by KO and lost 24.

If you're wondering why Max Baer is not on the list, the answer is simple. He was not Jewish, even though he wore a Star of David on his trunks and he was so described in publicity releases. The reason? To hypo the box office. According to the *Ring Record Book,* Baer was of German-Scotch descent.

Baer later went into show business, and his son, who is big enough for the heavyweight ranks, has continued the tradition—of acting, that is, not of fighting (he plays the burly son, Jethro, in "The Beverly Hillbillies"). Barney Ross also spent some time before the cameras. . . . There seems to be a lesson here, but I just can't put my finger on it. Maybe it's that there's more than one way to break into show biz. Hmmm. But by *boxing?*

To return to the business at hand—

Who were five great fighters of Italian descent?

Number 1 has to be Rocky Marciano (Francis Rocco Marchegiano), the only heavyweight champion undefeated in his entire career, with 49 straight victories, 43 by knockouts, and the last modern fighter to be ranked with the great old-timers. The Brockton Blockbuster was known for his dedication to training and his single-mindedness toward his goal of becoming world champ. He even delayed his marriage on the advice of his manager, Al Weill, until he had the title! In Philadelphia, on September 23, 1952, after trailing on points for 12 rounds, Rocky smashed Jersey Joe Walcott into submission in the 13th with a series of sledgehammer blows to annex the crown. He repeated the victory in shorter time in the rematch, in one round. He was knocked down only twice in his career. He retired on April 27, 1956—only the second heavyweight champ to do so (Gene Tunney was the first). Unlike almost all fighters, Rocky has to be admired for showing the good judgment to refrain from coming back despite lucrative offers. When asked why, he said: "I guess I'm not hungry any more."

Tony Canzoneri was twice lightweight champion and also featherweight and junior welterweight king (twice). He weighed only 95 pounds when he began boxing as a pro in 1925. He defeated Benny Bass in 1928 for the

166

featherweight title, and he knocked out Al Singer in the first round for the lightweight crown on November 14, 1930. He then started fighting as a junior welterweight and took the title from Jack ("Kid") Berg in 1931. Fighting in both classes, he lost the junior welter crown to Johnny Jadick in 1932 but regained it the following year from Battling Shaw. He remained lightweight king until

Barney Ross dethroned him in 1933. He ended a 15-year career when he was KO'd for the first and only time after 181 bouts by Al ("Bummy") Davis in the Garden on November 1, 1939.

Willie Pep (William Guglerimo Papaleo), featherweight champion, was a superb and ring-wise boxer. He compiled one of the most amazing winning streaks in ring history when he scored 62 triumphs in a row and won 134 of his first 136 fights. He was on top of the feather class for six years after taking the title from Chalky Wright in 1942. He lost it on a knockout to Sandy Saddler in 1948 but outpointed Saddler the next year to reclaim the crown. He had a total of 231 bouts in a busy 18 years in the ring.

Lou Ambers (Louis D'Ambrosio), lightweight champion, was known as the Herkimer Hurricane (he was born in Herkimer, N. Y.) for his rapid-fire punching. Another of the great lightweights of the 1930's, he took the title away from Tony Canzoneri on September 3, 1936, and kept it until Henry Armstrong outpointed him in 1938. He beat Armstrong in a rematch the next year. He lost the title to Lew Jenkins when he was counted out for the first time on May 10, 1940. After a second KO by Jenkins in 1941, he retired.

Fifth is Rocky Graziano (Thomas Rocco Barbella), a middleweight champion. He was a crowd-pleasing Pier Six battler whose title slugfests with Tony Zale were detailed earlier. Ray Robinson was the only other man to knock him out and Rocky had 52 kayos in 83 bouts! He retired in 1952 and enjoys success as a show-business and TV personality, specializing in commercials. His autobiography, *Somebody Up There Likes Me*, was made into a fine motion picture that launched the movie career of Paul Newman.

THE HUNGRY GLADIATORS

Here are a couple more Italian fighters you may never have heard of, but I can assure you they were among the greatest:

Johnny Dundee, who was baptized Joseph Corrara, was born in Shaikai, Italy, on November 22, 1892. Fans had much fun with his Scotch name, and you can imagine some of the nicknames he must have had. He is ranked as one of the top featherweights and he also met the leading lightweights of his time. Over a five-year span from 1915 to 1920 Dundee engaged in seven no-decision bouts with Benny Leonard! He started as a pro in 1910 and in 1913 battled Johnny Kilbane to a 20-round draw in Vernon, California, for the featherweight title. He won the junior lightweight crown from George Chaney on a foul in the fifth round in New York City on November 18, 1921, and held it for two years. After losing the title to Jack Bernstein on a 15-round decision on May 30, 1923, Dundee became the featherweight champion the next month by outpointing Eugene Criqui and then regained the junior lightweight title from Bernstein later in the year. He continued to be a headliner through the 1920's and was known for his skill in fighting off the ropes. A rugged campaigner, he boxed for almost 22 years before he finally retired in 1932. He had a total of 321 bouts, with 19 knockouts and 31 losses.

Young Corbett III, who was born Ralph Capabianca Giordano in Naples, Italy, on May 27, 1905, became one of the outstanding welterweights and also fought top-notch middleweights and light-heavyweights. He began as a pro in 1919 but his early record is incomplete. He got to the throne on February 22, 1933, when he decisioned Jack Fields (Jacob Finkelstein) in ten rounds at San Francisco, only to lose the welterweight title to Jimmy

169

McLarnin on May 29 of that year when he was kayoed in the first round. Among his notable victories afterward were a ten-round decision over Mickey Walker, a five-round knockout of Gus Lesnevich and a ten-round verdict over Billy Conn. After beating Fred Apostoli in a non-title match early in 1938, he lost in his bid for the middleweight title, held by Apostoli, later in the year. He quit in 1940 after 21 years and the incomplete records show that he had 71 bouts with 15 knockouts and eight losses.

Now, here's an easy category, for there have probably been more great Negro fighters than fighters from any other ethnic group.

Who were five great Negro fighters?

The greatest of them all, of course, was Joe Louis (Joe Louis Barrow), heavyweight champion. With KO power in each hand, he stalked his opponent relentlessly. As he once said of a foe (Tony Pastor), "He can run, but he can't hide." He set a record for number of title defenses (25) and was heavyweight king longer (from 1937 to 1949) than any other champion. He later attempted an ill-advised comeback. He only lost once before his retirement, suffering a 12th-round KO at the hands of Max Schmeling, which he later repaid with an awesome two-minute-four-second beating of the German. The Brown Bomber knocked out 54 men in 71 matches. Unschooled, he had the right instincts in and out of the ring. He donated two handsome purses from title bouts during World War II to the Army and Navy Relief Funds, and said: "I'm not fighting for nothing. I'm fighting for my country."

Henry Armstrong (Henry Jackson) was featherweight,

ightweight and welterweight champion. He alone held
all three titles at the same time. Noted for his perpetual
two-fisted windmill style of attack, he won his three titles
in less than ten months! First he belted out Petey Sarron
in six rounds at the Garden on October 29, 1937, for the
feather crown. Then he beat Barney Ross for the welter
title on May 31, 1938, and then Lou Ambers for the light-

171

weight crown on August 17, 1938. When he quit the ring in 1945 after 14 years, he had compiled a record of 97 knockouts in 175 bouts!

Ray Robinson (Walker Smith) was welterweight and middleweight champion. As a young boxer he was nicknamed Sugar because an onlooker said of his classic moves, "He's as sweet as sugar." He had a remarkable career extending for 24 years. He "retired" as often as Sarah Bernhardt did. He had a memorable six-bout series with rugged Jake LaMotta, winning five of them. He's the only boxer to hold the middleweight crown five times! Sugar Ray, often called the best boxer pound-for-pound in history, suffered only one "knockout" in his career. He fought Joey Maxim for the light-heavyweight title at Yankee Stadium on June 25, 1952, and collapsed from the heat after 13 rounds. Of 185 bouts, he scored 104 kayos, lost 13 by decision, had one draw and the "knockout" loss to Maxim.

Jack Johnson, heavyweight champion and all-time great, took over the title by knocking out Tommy Burns in Sydney, Australia, in the 14th round on December 26, 1908. Famed for his boxing skills, he is considered one of the finest feinters the sport has ever had and the possessor of the greatest left jab. He lost the title to Jess Willard in Havana in the 26th round on April 5, 1915, in a controversial ending. The suspicions were that he had "thrown" the bout. He continued to fight exhibitions in the early 1930's when he was in his fifties!

Fifth is Joe Gans, rated by many as the finest lightweight of all time, was born Joseph Gaines on November 25, 1874, in Baltimore. A clever boxer, he was known as the "Old Master." Starting as a pro in 1891, he rapidly rose into the limelight, although the records are incomplete on his early years. He finally got his chance for the world lightweight title when he was matched with Frank Erne on March 23, 1900, in New York, but an injury prevented Gans from continuing after the 12th round. He was not able to get another bout with Erne until May 12, 1902, and he kayoed Erne in the first round. He also fought welterweights and held Joe Walcott, the champion, to a 20-round draw on September 30, 1904, in San Francisco. He remained the lightweight king for six years until he was knocked out in the 17th round by Battling Nelson on July 4, 1908. He lost again to Nelson and had only one bout in 1909 before retiring. A year later he died of tuberculosis in Baltimore on August 10, 1910. For his almost 20 years in the ring, his bouts that are in the record book credit him with 55 knockouts in 156 matches and only eight losses.

One more (among many, many others) is Sam Langford, the Boston Tar Baby, who was regarded as one of the greater fighters although he never held a title. He began as a featherweight in 1902 and fought up to heavyweights even though he never scaled more than 180 pounds. One memorable match was with Jack Johnson in 1906 in which Langford lost a 15-round decision. Johnson said he never wanted to fight him again. Jack Dempsey also ducked him. Which helps explain why he never won the heavyweight title. He was boxing until 1924, when he was 44 years old. In all he had 252 bouts, with 99 knockouts.

Now it seems that it's the Puerto Ricans' turn to climb the fistic heights. All the evidence isn't in yet, but what there is points to them as producing some of the greatest fighters of the modern era. What other nationality group of comparable size can boast two present world champions: Jose Torres, the light-heavyweight king, and Carlos

Ortiz, the lightweight titleholder? But whatever the final outcome, the Puerto Ricans have begun that upward struggle.

10

The Pastures Get Greener

TODAY's professional golfers play for such fabulous purses and are the objects of so much adulation that it's hard to believe they once were second-class citizens. In the old days in Scotland and England the pros had to change clothes and eat in the pro shop—if there was one—while the amateur contestants were enjoying the plush facilities of the clubhouse. Even after that situation was remedied the discrimination continued in one form or another for several years. In fact, until about 1930 the amateurs in an open tournament always were listed with a "Mr." in front of their names, while Joe Blow, the pro, was on the program as plain old Joe Blow. If you're a pre-television golf fan perhaps you know who was responsible for the elimination of such unfair practices.

Which American golfer almost singlehandedly gained equal rights for professionals?

Walter Hagen. When the Haig went to Britain in 1920 for his first crack at the British Open, he found the club-

house closed to him. He was told to dress in the shop of Mr. Hunter, the professional, and there he found the "facilities" to be a peg on the wall and a pile of shoes in the corner. Hagen, who always went first class, chose to change clothes in his rented limousine rather than submit to such an indignity. The next week, when he went to Paris for the French Open, he encountered the same situation. This time he bristled and, with the reluctant support of two top British pros, he threatened to withdraw if not allowed to eat and dress in the clubhouse. The officials gave in and, thanks to Hagen, the pros soon had equal, if not exalted, status.

THE PASTURES GET GREENER

Another feature of present-day golf that had its origin many years ago, is the term Grand Slam. Nowadays, whenever an Arnold Palmer or Jack Nicklaus wins the Masters in April, he immediately announces he will shoot for the Grand Slam. Today this means the U. S. Open, British Open and Professional Golfers' Association championship, in addition to the Masters. However, the original Grand Slam was something different. How much do you know about it?

Who completed the original Grand Slam, what tournaments were involved, and when was it accomplished?

Bobby Jones won the Grand Slam in 1930 by taking the U. S. Open, British Open, U. S. Amateur and British Amateur titles in that year. Although Jones's feat was tremendous and may never be duplicated, it was something people predicted he might accomplish, so great were his abilities. In fact, in the seven years before 1930 Jones had won three U. S. Opens, four U. S. Amateurs and two British Opens, so he certainly was no stranger to the winner's circle. He started off by winning the British Amateur, which he had never won previously and which he considered the most difficult of the four because the matches were only 18 holes right through the final. By contrast, the semifinals and final of the U. S. Amateur were 36 holes and Jones felt this gave him more room to cope with any opponent who might be having a hot round. Where the Amateur victory at St. Andrews had been touched by destiny, the Open at Hoylake was hard work and Jones had to struggle to win by two strokes with 291. Back home two weeks later, at Interlachen, Jones

177

took command in the U. S. Open with a third-round 68 and coasted home by two shots at 287. The final event, the U. S. Amateur at Merion, was a triumphal procession. Jones had no match closer than 5 and 4, and beat Gene Homans in the final, 8 and 7.

Jones retired after completing the Slam. He was only 28 years old, but he had won 13 major championships in eight years. His feat may never be duplicated because (1) players of his ability don't come along every day and (2) he was an amateur throughout his career. Today's golfers turn pro so fast they don't have time to pursue the amateur championships.

Since 1930 only two golfers have done anything that approached what Jones accomplished. Can you remember who they were?

Which golfer won the U. S. and British Amateurs in 1934, then did the same thing in 1935?

Lawson Little. Little, a great player, completed his double-double by winning 31 consecutive matches. He then turned pro and, although he later won the U. S. Open, he never quite attained the heights predicted for him after his amateur successes.

Which golfer won the Masters, U. S. Open and British Open in 1953?

Ben Hogan. Hogan was one of the greatest golfers of all time. His performance in 1953 is all the more amazing when you consider that in 1949 he nearly lost his life in an automobile accident that almost crippled him for life. Yet despite his aching legs and the rigors of playing those 36-

hole matches in tournament play, he won the U. S. Open three times in four years after coming back from the accident.

The most remarkable of Hogan's victories in 1953 was the British Open at Carnoustie. He went over to England only because friends told him it would be a shame for a player of his caliber to retire without ever taking a shot at the oldest of championships. He expected to win and everyone else expected it, too, so the pressure was tremendous. Despite the cold, the wind, the rain and the colossal fatigue, Hogan did win and set a course record of 68 in the final round. The Scots, who take the game seriously, were reserved at first, but they soon took to their hearts the man who probably took golf more seriously than anyone who ever lived.

Although most golfers hope to gain lasting fame by winning the U. S. Open, one man became famous at least in part because he didn't win it. Do you remember his name?

Which golfer has won well over 100 tournaments but has never won the U. S. Open?

Sam Snead. The famous West Virginia hillbilly won the P.G.A. three times, the Masters three times and the British Open once, but he never won the U. S. Open in 25 tries, although he finished second four times. Snead finished second in his first attempt, in 1937, and was among the favorites for the next 20 years. In 1939 he suffered his most tragic failure and many persons feel that if he had won that one he might have gone on to take the Open several times. On that occasion he came to the last hole needing a par five to win and a bogey six to tie—and he took a staggering eight and finished fourth. He tied for first in 1947, losing in a playoff to Lew Worsham, and finished second to Hogan in 1953.

Another one of golf's all-time heroes once put together a string of victories that, considering today's large number of capable players, probably won't be matched. Can you recall him?

THE PASTURES GET GREENER

Which golfer once won 13 consecutive tournaments and finished in the money in 114 straight?

Byron Nelson. Nelson compiled his records during 1944 and 1945 and many are prone to discount his performances because of the lack of competition during the war. However, there still was Old Man Par to beat, and beat him Nelson did. In 1945 he won a total of 19 tournaments and averaged 68.33 strokes per round, a fantastic achievement!

Unlike most sports, the most cherished feat in golf—the hole-in-one—is in reach of the rankest amateur. And the fact that almost 15,000 aces were reported in 1965 is proof that some pretty rank players must have got lucky. Indeed, luck has to be considered the chief factor, since most of the leading pros have never had more than one or two aces and many have yet to get their first. There is, however, one exception. How much do you know about aces in general and about the man who has scored the greatest number?

What are the odds against making a hole-in-one? What is the longest hole-in-one on record?

The odds are more than a million to one, so if you never get an ace, don't feel too badly. Despite these odds, Robert Mitera of Omaha, Nebraska, knocked his tee shot into the cup on the 444-yard tenth hole at the Miracle Hills Golf Club in Omaha on October 7, 1965. The previous longest had been 427 yards by Lou Kretlow, the former major league pitcher. The man with the most is Art Wall,

Jr., the 1959 Masters champion, who has 35 to his credit. Wall grew up in Honesdale, Pennsylvania, and got 22 aces on his local course, where he used to play 36 to 54 holes daily as a youngster. He has had two aces in P.G.A. tour events.

Although some pro usually gets a hole-in-one every week on the tour, the most famous single shots in golf have not been aces. One that comes to mind was a wedge shot that traveled a little over 100 yards and earned the man who hit it something in the neighborhood of $50,000. Can you remember the circumstances?

Which player won George May's World Championship in 1953 by hitting a wedge shot for an eagle on the final hole?

Lew Worsham. Chandler Harper was standing near the 18th green with a victory smile on his face as Worsham prepared to hit his approach. The 1947 U. S. Open champion needed a birdie three to tie and the odds were against him getting it. Naturally, the idea that he might get a two and win didn't cross anyone's mind. However, he did just that and won the $25,000 first prize plus an equal amount for playing a series of exhibitions. Since second prize was worth $10,000, Worsham's shot made him $40,000. A year or so later the prize money was doubled and subsequent winners of the "World" title earned $100,000.

Another famous shot was made by a man who already was famous when it happened, although he is best remembered by many for that single stroke. You can have two clues on this one.

THE PASTURES GET GREENER

*Which player won the 1932 U. S. Open by playing the
last 28 holes in 100 strokes?*

Gene Sarazen. Gene has to be the most durable figure
in golf. He broke in around 1920 when still a teenager
and, in the next 15 years, won two U. S. Opens, three
P.G.A. championships, the British Open and the Masters,
plus dozens of other tournaments all over the world. He
tied for the U. S. Open in 1940, losing in a playoff, and
was still shooting sub-par golf when he was in his fifties.
Today, still a good golfer, he can be seen every week on a
television golf series, easily recognizable in his stylish
plus-fours.

On the final day of the 1932 Open at Fresh Meadow,
Gene shot the last ten holes of the third round in 34
strokes, then went out that afternoon and shot a 66 to win.
Three years later, he sank a 220-yard spoon shot for a
double eagle that gave him a tie for the Masters, which he
won in a playoff with Craig Wood the next day.

Although Sarazen never seems to change, other aspects
of golf are considerably different. Perhaps the biggest
change has been in the clubs themselves. Back in the days
of the hickory shaft and the stymie, clubs had names
instead of numbers. It wasn't until manufacturers began
to turn out matched sets of steel-shafted clubs that the
current numbering system came into being. Most people
today still use the names driver, brassie and spoon to
denote the Nos. 1, 2 and 3 woods, but how about all those
other colorful names of Scottish origin that so enriched
the history of the game? Here are some examples:

What is a mashie? What is a niblick? What is a midiron?

A mashie was a No. 5 iron, a niblick a No. 9 iron and a midiron a No. 2 iron. And there were others, such as baffy and cleek, to give the game a touch of color it could use today. In the old days, players carried only six or seven clubs (in fact, Chick Evans carried only seven in winning the 1916 U. S. Open), but as the demand for more clubs grew, new names had to be invented. Thus, the mashie-niblick, being a combination of the Nos. 5 and 9, was the forerunner of today's No. 7 iron.

Something else that is changing, unnecessarily it seems to me, is the format of the major championships. The U. S. Open has done away with its traditional 36-hole grind on Saturday and the U. S. Amateur and P.G.A. championship have been changed from match play to medal. Most golfers contend, no doubt correctly, that medal play is the truest test of a golfer, but following two great tacticians through a 36-hole match is one of the great experiences of golf and can never be equaled in a stroke-play tournament.

There have been many great match-play golfers down through the years, but one of them was so good that he has to be listed at the top. Maybe you can remember him.

Which golfer won the P.G.A. championship five times when it was at match play?

Walter Hagen. The Haig, who left his mark on all phases of the game, won his first P.G.A. title in 1921, was runnerup in 1923, then won four straight from 1924 through 1927. He reached the quarterfinals in 1928 and the semifinals in 1929, losing both times to Leo Diegel, who won the title both years. Hagen not only was a great player, but a master of psychological warfare and he outsmarted many an opponent and won even on days when his game wasn't sharp. He was a remarkable scrambler and one of the five or six greatest putters who ever stepped on a green. Many a foe, on the green with a sure par and a possible birdie, would be completely undone

when Hagen would make an impossible shot to the green from the rough, then sink a long putt.

Among the constants in golf—or any other sport—are the inexplicable last-minute collapses and the come-from-behind finishes. The old saw about the game not being over till the last man is out applies to golf, too. One of the most notable about-faces in recent years occurred at the Masters when the eventual winner made up nine strokes on the final round. Do you remember the players involved?

Which golfer took a four-stroke lead into the final round of the 1956 Masters only to shoot a closing 80 and finish a stroke behind?

Ken Venturi. Venturi has always had an affinity for the Masters, which he has never won, and this defeat has stayed with him through the years, only partly atoned for when he won the U. S. Open in 1964. He began the last round at Augusta four shots ahead of Cary Middlecoff, while Jack Burke, Jr., was eight behind. In the final 18 holes, Burke shot 71, Middlecoff 77 and Venturi 80. It should be noted that Venturi's 80 was not all the fault of bad golf. Playing conditions were bad and there were many high scores that day. Burke's 71 was the lowest score of the round. Venturi also appeared to have won the 1960 Masters, but Arnold Palmer birdied the last two holes to win by a stroke.

To take an opposite case, one famous golfer overcame a seven-stroke deficit on the final round of the 1960 U. S. Open and won by two strokes. At lunch between the third and fourth rounds, this man was asked what he thought he would have to do to overtake the leaders and he replied that a score of 65 should do it. Thereupon he went out and shot the 65, with the help of a 30 on the front nine. Do you remember the occasion?

Which golfer won the 1960 U. S. Open with a closing 65 after starting the round seven shots behind?

Arnold Palmer. Arnie has won a lot of tournaments with stirring finishes, but this was the one that made his reputation. Mike Souchak was leading after three rounds and Palmer was back in a tie for 15th place. But with that outgoing 30 Arnie passed people by twos and fours and won going away. Jack Nicklaus, who was still an amateur, finished second. Souchak, who has never been able to keep his game going through a major championship, closed with a 75 and tied for third.

A friend of mine once described Arnold Palmer as the "Barbra Streisand of golf." The description may not seem very apt at first (since Arnie's been in the public eye a lot longer than Miss Streisand, it might be more fitting to say that she is the Arnold Palmer of show business), but when you consider it you can see what he meant. For Arnie Palmer has that special something, that charisma, that "star quality" which draws people wherever he goes. Even during a lackluster tournament campaign, "Arnie's Army" will line the fairways, attending to their hero and ignoring the fellow a couple of holes away who may be burning up the course.

But there's another reason for the fascination Arnie holds for his army of admirers. I remember following Arnie around the course at Pebble Beach, California, with his charming wife Winnie. On a long par-4 hole Arnie was just off the green on two. Instead of making a safe chip

shot and setting up an easy par, Arnie hit dead for the pin, and overshot the green. Coming back he again hit for the pin, but this time the ball caught and he was lucky to come away from the hole with a double bogey. Winnie Palmer turned to me and said: "You'd think that once— just *once*—he'd settle for par."

Arnold Palmer won't settle for par, and that's the only reason he's gotten everything that's come his way. A millionaire businessman, he could quit the game any time he feels like it, or loaf through the tournament round if his ego won't allow him to quit, but no, Arnie goes out every day like a hungry youngster, ready to take on all comers and never settling for par. And the crowd continues to follow him because they know that, whether Arnie wins or loses, they are going to see some exciting golf.

The international aspect of golf has always fascinated me. Sometimes professional golfers remind me of a band of gypsies, men without countries whose only homes are isolated patches of green to which they drop from out of the sky. To wind up this chapter, then, here are some challenges concerned with foreign golfers.

Foreign golfers have left their mark in this country off and on for more than 60 years, but never have they been involved more significantly than in the 1913 U. S. Open, perhaps the most historic tournament in this country's history. How much do you remember about it?

Which unknown amateur surprised the golfing world by winning the 1913 U. S. Open?

Francis Ouimet defeated Harry Vardon and Ted Ray in a playoff for the championship. Ouimet, who had gained some notice in his home area, had to be talked into entering the Open at Brookline. Certainly no one—including Ouimet—thought he had a chance. Vardon and Ray were two of the best golfers in the world and the only American given a shot at them in pre-tourney speculation was Johnny McDermott, who had won the Open the previous two years. Vardon, although slightly past his prime, had six British Opens to his credit and had won the U. S. Open on his first visit here in 1900. Ray, one of the game's longest hitters, had won one British Open and was at the height of his career (he later won the U. S. Open in 1920, and Vardon lost it tragically at the age of 50). Anyway, Ouimet played very well in the rain the final day and tied the two Britons. Then, in the playoff the next day, he shot a 72 and trounced his foes. Vardon shot a 77 and Ray a 78. This was the Open that put golf on America's front pages and showed that we could, at last, hold our own with the British. Ouimet later won two U. S. Amateurs, captained several Walker Cup teams and was the first American to become captain of the Royal and Ancient Golf Club at St. Andrews.

Other foreign golfers, from Harold Hilton to Bobby Locke, have been successful here, but one invader stands out above the rest. Do you know who he is?

Which golfer won the Masters in 1961 to become the first foreigner to do so?

Gary Player. This intense little South African first attracted notice by finishing second in the 1958 U. S. Open. Since then he has been considered a member of the Big Three with Palmer and Nicklaus. He showed another side of his character when he gave away his entire first-place check of $25,000 after winning the Open in 1965. The bulk of the money was earmarked for junior golf, while a portion went to cancer research. Player watches his diet, does exercises to strengthen his muscles so he can drive the ball as far as the big boys, and generally works harder at the game than most. His quiet assurance, his politeness and his British accent have combined to make him extremely popular in this country.

Besides the major championships, the most important golfing events are the biennial matches played between

$25,000

...IT'S ONLY MONEY!

teams representing Great Britain and the United States. Are you familiar with them?

For what famous cups do British and American golfers play?

The pros compete for the Ryder Cup, which was donated by Samuel Ryder, a British seed merchant. The competition began in 1927 and the United States has lost only three matches since that time.

The men amateurs compete for the Walker Cup, which was named for George H. Walker, who was president of the U. S. Golf Association when the idea was conceived.

The first match was held in 1922 at the National Golf Links of America at Southampton, Long Island, and one of the four points scored by the losing British side was gained by a man who wasn't even a member of the team. Robert Harris was the British captain, but he fell ill the night before the matches and was replaced by Bernard Darwin, the great English golf writer, who was covering the competition for The Times of London. Darwin lost the first three holes of his singles match, then rallied to win, 3 and 1. The Americans have lost only one match since that first one in 1922.

The women amateurs play for the Curtis Cup, which was donated by Margaret and Harriot Curtis, sisters who were major figures in American women's golf in the early years of the century. The matches were first played in 1932 and the Americans have lost only twice.

Although scoring records in golf aren't as meaningful as in some other sports (for example, a 68 on your local public course is a lot easier to attain than a 68 at Augusta National), still they are impressive and some of them are worth remembering. How many do you recall?

What is the lowest 72-hole score posted in a P.G.A. event?

Mike Souchak set the 72-hole mark at 257 in winning the 1955 Texas Open at Brackenridge Park in San Antonio. He shot a 27 on the second nine of the opening round to set a record for nine holes and finished the round with a 60 to tie the mark held by Al Brosch, Bill Nary, Ted Kroll, Wally Ulrich, Tommy Bolt and Sam Snead. He went on to shoot 68, 64, and 65 for the 257.

THE PASTURES GET GREENER

Which golfer scored the most consecutive birdies in a tournament?

Bob Goalby had eight straight birdies during the fourth round of the 1961 St. Petersburg Open.

What is the fewest number of putts used in a tournament round?

Bill Nary and Bob Rosburg share the mark for fewest putts in a round with 19. Nary did it at El Paso in 1952 and Rosburg at Pensacola in 1959.

I'd be remiss if, in closing, I didn't add a note about a friend whom all golfers will miss . . . Tony Lema, who was killed in an airplane crash in August 1966. They called him "Champagne Tony," and it was an apt nickname, for he was a sparkling, unforgettable human being. You had to meet him but once to know that here was a *man!* He enjoyed life and lived it to the fullest. I don't want to make this sound like a eulogy . . . it's just that I really liked Tony as a golfer and as a human being.

11

Aces at the Net

THERE are two schools of thought about the current state of tennis. One—the old school—feels that the game has degenerated into nothing more than a sideshow in which two giants stand at opposite sides of a net and try to kill each other with bullet-like services. There is no strategy, they say, there is no longer the thrill of an extended rally, a sensational save—in short, there is no longer any *fun* in the game. There is a lot of truth in what these people say, for if you've ever watched the modern game as it is played by the top amateurs and the pros you must have noticed a remarkable sameness in the matches.

The other school—the modern school—replies that the old game of tennis is dead. Sure there were the great stars such as Tilden and Johnston, but the game as a popular sport that caught the imagination of the public died with their passing. What the game needs is a new breed of superstars who are professional, motivated (that is, paid) to win, and who will devote their full time to the sport just

like any other professional athlete, using all the techniques of training and conditioning that are used in other sports. If the result of this is a lightning-fast game requiring perfect reflexes and deadly accuracy, so much the better. And whether boring or not, the fans have been coming back to the game in increasing numbers.

This is the sort of argument I like to stay out of, but I will say this: One of the main reasons people attend sporting events is the same reason they attend the opera or the ballet or whatever—to see somebody do something better than they can do themselves. Keeping this in mind, I'd be inclined to side with the modern point of view, because I don't think anyone will disagree with me when I say that

195

a player like Gonzalez is a joy to watch, and as long as there are players like him—and *only* as long as there are players like him—the sport will have its popularity with spectators.

Now that I've gotten out of that one (or have I?), let's try some challenges. I don't get too many questions concerned with tennis on my program, but that doesn't stop me from throwing a few at *you*.

Who is the only man to have won the Wimbledon singles championship three times?

Fred Perry of Britain did it in 1934, 1935 and 1936, beating Jack Crawford of Australia in the final once and Baron Gottfried von Cramm of Germany twice for the world's most important championship.

How many players have accomplished tennis's Grand Slam—winning the Australian, French, British and American championships?

Only two. Don Budge of the United States, in 1938, and Rod Laver of Australia, in 1962. At the beginning of his career, around 1933, Budge became convinced that to do well in the big time he would have to do something about his forehand—his backhand was one of the most lethal in the history of the game. Accordingly, in his typical bulldog fashion, he went back home to California and spent a year with a coach working on the stroke. It was only after he had done that necessary job that he was able to attain greatness. Laver was a link in the chain of super stars developed by Harry Hopman, the famous Australian coach, that included Ken Rosewall, Lew Hoad, Frank

Sedgman and Neale Fraser. Laver was taken out of school at 16 to concentrate on tennis and developed such a powerful game that even when he turned pro, it did not take him long to dominate the field.

How did the Davis Cup originate?

The late Dwight Davis, then a 21-year-old senior at Harvard and an enthusiast of the game, spent $800 in 1900 for the trophy that has assumed his name. He intended the cup for an international competition, to be kept by victorious nations. Under the rules, the nation that wins the cup holds it for a year, then meets the nation that survives an elimination tournament in what is called the challenge round. (Luckily, you can't copyright titles.) In cup play, there are four singles matches and a doubles match. To win, a nation must take three of the five matches.

Which nation has won the Davis Cup most times?

Australia, which has won the cup 20 times. The United States has won it 19 times, Britain nine times and France six times. France dominated cup play from 1927 through 1932, when the Four Musketeers—Henri Cochet, Jean Borotra, Jacques Brugnon and Rene Lacoste—were in their glory. After World War II, however, Australia has won 13 times and the U. S. seven.

What was the Golden Era of tennis?

From 1920 to 1930, the sports pages were filled with the names of Bill Tilden, Billy Johnston, Vinnie Richards and

R. Norris Williams. The ballyhoo over their matches across the country created thousands of fans. In 1926 a match was played that put tennis on the front pages; it was between Suzanne Lenglen of France, called the greatest woman player in the world, and Helen Wills, the all-American girl—calm, cool and efficient. Suzanne won, 6–3, 8–6, although Helen nearly evened matters in the second set. But it gave tennis a tremendous impetus. The loser became "Our Helen" and "Queen Helen," the biggest drawing card in the game except for Tilden. The

ACES AT THE NET

Four Musketeers from France then appeared on the scene and began to close in on America's best. Lacoste beat Tilden in 1926 and led his compatriots to victory the following year by beating both Tilden and Johnston. The French then started a long reign of Davis Cup supremacy.

Who is the most successful Davis Cup coach in history?

Harry Hopman of Australia. His formula: intensive physical training and emphasis on the theory of "hitting for the lines." Hopman's abrasive personality has made him many enemies, particularly among the press, but his pupils swear by him. Among the stars he has developed are Frank Sedgman, Ken McGregor, Lew Hoad, Ken Rosewall, Neale Fraser and Rod Laver.

How many years did Bill Tilden rank first in the U. S.?

Ten years, from 1919 through 1929, after which he turned pro. He won the U. S. singles title seven times. No other player in the modern era has even approached those records. Tilden was colorful, controversial and a complete tennis player. Many experts rate him as the greatest the game has ever known.

Who was the most dominant figure in U. S. women's tennis?

Helen Wills, who ranked first seven times and won the singles title seven times, the last time in 1931. Two years later, in 1933, she made a comeback and reached the final with Helen Jacobs. With the score 8–6, 3–6, 3–0 against her, she paused dramatically on the court, walked to the umpire's chair and said with her characteristic poker face: "Please tell my opponent I am unable to continue because of a strained back." There was no love lost between the two stars and Miss Jacobs, who had won the title the previous year, was to go on to take it a total of four times.

Whatever happened to "Little Mo" Connolly?

Maureen Connolly, a short, sturdily built girl, had extraordinary power in her ground strokes. She won the U. S. singles title in 1951, 1952 and 1953, the last person to do so three times in a row (others who did it before were Pauline Betz, Alice Marble, Margaret Osborne, Helen Wills and Molla Mallory). Ranked No. 10 in 1950, she shot up to No. 1 the following year and stayed there through 1953, when a riding accident forced her to retire.

What was the biggest crowd ever to see a Davis Cup tennis match?

About 26,000 turned out at Kooyong Stadium in Melbourne, Australia, in 1953, when Australia defeated the United States, 3–2, in the challenge round. Wimbledon, site of the British championship, has drawn up to 30,000 in a day of play. The Forest Hills stadium in Queens, scene of the United States nationals, has a capacity of 14,500, which has often been exceeded.

What has been the major change in tennis since the days of Tilden, Budge, Riggs, Perry, Von Cramm?

There was more baseline play in those days. Today, a player goes to the net regularly behind his serve and tries to put the ball away with his volley for the point. This serve-volley pattern has been copied so avidly that many fans feel it is producing boring tennis. Yet it is skillful, winning tennis, and, as I said before, as long as it pays off in victories and the rules are not altered, it will continue to be practiced by major players.

Why are some players better on a grass court and others on a clay court?

The difference is in the bounce and spin as the ball strikes the surface. A big server has the advantage on grass because his ball skids as it hits, forcing a weak return that he should be able to put away. On clay, his serve is not nearly so effective because the ball will "come up" after striking the surface. On grass, it is dangerous to stay on the baseline because of the peril of bad bounces, so the idea is to get the commanding position at the net as soon as possible. On clay, the movement of the ball is slower, thus making it easier to retrieve shots. Steadiness and patience are required to win a clay match—that is, being able to keep the ball in play from the backcourt and having the patience to wait for the right approach to the net. The volleyer is more vulnerable to the passing shot on clay, as the ball will "hang" and allow his opponent the time to put it by him.

What is the Wightman Cup?

It is a trophy donated by the "all-time great," Hazel Hotchkiss Wightman, for a women's competition between England and the United States. The series began in 1923 and is played annually. Three women on each team play a total of five singles matches and there are two doubles matches, making a total of seven matches. Over the years England has won six times and the U. S. 31.

In tennis, as in other sports, the big man has the advantage. But there have been some notable exceptions.

Are there any small tennis players who have become great champions?

Yes. Bryan ("Bitsy") Grant of Atlanta, who was in the top 10 from 1933 to 1941, except 1940. Grant was five feet six inches tall and stayed on top of the game through his remarkable retrieving ability. His steadiness discouraged his opponents; they could not get the ball past him. He was a master at strategy and in the use of spin and drop shots; he was also a superb doubles player. Another is Ken Rosewall (five-eight), the master of control and possessor of what is generally considered the best backhand in the game. An artist in both the backcourt and forecourt, quick and clever, he took over the professional championship from Pancho Gonzalez. Now coming up is Joaquin Layo-Mayo of Mexico, who's five-six.

How many great players have two-handed shots?

The best today is Cliff Drysdale of South Africa, who has remarkable control of his two-handed backhand and uses it to score heavily. Mike Belkin of Miami Beach, ranked seventh in the U. S., also hits his backhand with the two-fisted grip. Pancho Segura of Ecuador whaled the ball with two hands from both forehand and backhand, and was so good that he was able to earn a world ranking in the early 1940's. Billy Lenoir of Arizona and Jim Mc-

Manus of California are others with two-fisted backhands. In the 1930's, Vivian McGrath and Jack Bromwich of Australia were the greatest exponents of that style. Bromwich, especially, was a master in doubles, as he had a talent for disguising his shots.

Many people, especially the uninitiated, are dismayed over the complexity of the scoring system in tennis. All those aces and deuces and ads and loves. But something is now being done about it.

What is VASSS?

It is the Van Alen Simplified Scoring System devised by James Van Alen of Newport, Rhode Island, the president of the Tennis Hall of Fame. The system is based primarily on the table tennis idea of scoring, and therefore there are no deuces and ads. A match consists of 31 points. The chief aim of VASSS is to shorten matches. The pros have adopted the system in the belief that it produces more exciting tennis for the spectators. There have been only a few amateur VASSS tournaments, as the U.S.L.T.A. officials have shown a cool attitude toward the system. Van Alen has been plugging it for six years and is determined to put it across for what he calls the betterment of the game.

This next question may seem frivolous, but it appears to be the one subject that interests my lady listeners. Incidentally, I've heard it said many times that tennis is the one sport that sets off the male physique to perfection. There's something about those white togs that make the ladies flip. Maybe that explains its continuing popularity as a participant sport.

How many of the top players in the U. S. are married?

Dennis Ralston (No. 1), Chuck McKinley (4), Ham Richardson (6), Marty Riessen (8) and Ron Holmberg (9). Among the second ten, Frank Froehling, Clark Graebner and Billy Lenoir. Arthur Ashe (2) is engaged, which leaves as holdouts: Cliff Richey, Charlie Pasarell, Tom Edlefsen. Four of the top ten women are married: Billie Jean King, Carole Graebner, Carol Aucamp and Donna Fales.

Of course, those tennis togs don't do the ladies any harm either. In fact, there was one female player who was more famous for her outfit than for her tennis.

Was Gussie Moran really a good player?

The general consensus is that Gussie, who ranked fourth in the U. S. in 1948, and is now in radio-TV, had one of the most solid games in women's tennis. She was three times in the top ten, and was always a graceful player to watch. To put it mildly.

Who was a player who rose to fame despite having diabetes?

Billy Talbert. Helped by insulin injections and pills and special exercises, the Cincinnati-born star played for many years in top competition, gaining a high ranking. Talbert had to modify his game to cope with his ailment. He knew that he would weaken in long matches, so he developed an effort-saving style; for instance, he was famous for his short-swing serve and the economy of his ground stroking. The highest ranking he achieved was third in 1949, but he was unsurpassed as a doubles player, winning the national crown with Gar Mulloy four times. He went on to captain the Davis Cup team, although he fell in disfavor with the bigwigs because of his independence. Today he is regarded as the elder statesman of tennis because of his experience as a player and his thorough knowledge of the game.

Here is the question that is probably asked the most about modern tennis:

Why has Australia emerged as such a dominant tennis nation?

Australia has a tremendous number of courts in ratio to population. Tennis is the country's national game and is played day and night. Promising young players are taken in hand by coaches and officials and given every opportunity to improve; this is part of an all-encompassing junior program that is the envy of other nations. When Margaret Smith, the world's ranking woman player, started to learn the game, she had only to step outside her house to have a choice of 40 grass courts on which to practice. When the American astronauts flew over Australia at night, the lights from tennis courts caught their attention. Good coaching has also played an important role in the development of Aussie stars. Harry Hopman, the Davis Cup captain, is recognized all over the world as one of the best coaches in the game.

Do top singles players make good doubles players?

Not necessarily. The reason is that doubles play requires a more varied repertory of shots, in addition to calling for teamwork and special strategy. For success in doubles, the two players must learn to blend their talent so that they may present the strongest front while attacking and defending. Each must be ready to sacrifice himself for the good of the team. The serve, volley and over-head are the three most important weapons in doubles, and it is usually the team that is "hitting down" not "up" that comes out on top. Among the great doubles teams have been the aforementioned Talbert and Mulloy; Don Budge and Gene Mako; George Lott and Johnny Doeg (Lott won the U. S. doubles title a record total of five times, twice with Les Stoefen, twice with Johnny Doeg and once with John Hennessey, who was once said to have played a "perfect" set—that is, without a single error); Bill Tilden and Vinnie Richards (although Tilden was said to have disliked doubles); Jack Kramer and Ted Schroeder; John Bromwich and Frank Sedgman of Australia; Neale Fraser and Roy Emerson of Australia; Chuck McKinley and Dennis Ralston, who won the U. S. title 3 times; and Ken Rosewall and Lew Hoad of Australia.

What were Pauline Betz's accomplishments?

At the start of World War II, Miss Betz was only 20. She won the U. S. title in 1942, 1943 and 1944, and again in 1946; in 1945 she was beaten in the final by Sarah Palfrey Cooke in what many people considered the greatest women's match ever seen—3–6, 8–6, 6–4. In 1946, when she was not quite 27, she went to Wimbledon for the first—and only—time and won that title. That year she also stood out in the very powerful U. S. Wightman Cup team that included Margaret Osborne, Louise Brough and Doris Hart. Between them, they won 23 of the Big Four singles championships. Miss Betz turned pro in 1947, with her peak period restricted by the war. As Mrs. Addie, with four children and past 40, she played a great match with Althea Gibson, taking her to 7–5 in the third set. With her extraordinary court-covering ability, her magnificent backhand and her ability to play a scrambling game, it is generally agreed she would have been a test for any top women player in history.

Whatever happened to Art Larsen?

The blond Californian, a tough player who won the U. S. singles title in 1950, beating Herbie Flam of Los Angeles in the final, 6–3, 4–6, 5–7, 6–4, 6–3, became involved in a terrible motor scooter accident shortly afterward. He lost the sight of an eye and suffered part paralysis on the left side. Of course it meant the end of his tennis career. However, he made good progress toward recovering and is currently attending Cal State College, studying journalism. Occasionally he works out with the school tennis team.

What is the outstanding brother-sister act in big-time tennis today?

The exploits of Cliff and Nancy Richey of San Angelo, Texas. Cliff ranks third in the U. S. and is fiercely dedicated to becoming No. 1 in the world. His father, a coach, took him out of high school for a year so he could get experience on the world circuit. Nancy, co-ranked No. 1 with Mrs. Billie Jean King, is three years older than Cliff and stands high in the world ratings. The two are sharply different personalities. Cliff has been involved in many tempestuous outbreaks on the court, but Nancy is placid. They never play doubles together because, as each has said, "it just doesn't work."

What is the Federation Cup?

It is the women's version of the Davis Cup, originating in 1963. In the four years it has been played, the U. S. has won twice and Australia twice. In 1966, the matches were held in Turin, Italy, with 16 nations competing. The U. S. team, consisting of Mrs. King, Julie Heldman and Carole

Graebner, defeated Germany in the final. Australia had been favored, but suffered a setback when her top star, Margaret Smith, was injured and unable to play. The matches consist of 2 singles and a doubles.

Who was the last American to win the U. S. men's singles championship?

Tony Trabert of Cincinnati, in 1955. Since then the following foreigners have won: Ken Rosewall, Mal Anderson, Ashley Cooper, Neale Fraser (twice in a row), Roy Emerson, Rod Laver—all of Australia; Rafael Osuna of Mexico (who downed Frank Froehling of the U. S. in a remarkable final by standing five feet behind the baseline and lobbing every ball back to his frantic opponent); Emerson and Manuel Santana of Spain. From 1937 through 1950, no foreigner was able to take the title.

12

How Fast and How High Can
They Go?

If you've never been in a sports debate comparing the present-day stars with the stars of the past, then you're no sports fan, because that's the heart of the whole thing. It's got to come that way. Once you've finished debating who's better, Koufax or Marichal, then you've got to get to the marrow—who's better, Koufax or Hubbell, Koufax or Grove, Koufax or Johnson, Koufax or . . . you name him.

At WNBC we had a "Dream World Series" broadcast. The fans picked the all-time stars of the National League and the American League, and then we had a playoff. How? By computer. It's come to that, which is not too surprising, because when you compare the past and the present, what have you got to go by but records and averages, which can be easily stored by a machine. But it has always seemed to me that there is a better way to compare athletes of different eras—by the watch and the tape measure. The heart and the eyes may lie; the watch and the tape can't. And don't give me that bit about how it's the human who controls them. You'd be surprised how objective those officials can be. Give a man a badge and a watch and all nostalgia goes by the boards.

One afternoon I received a call from one of my young listeners. "Look, Bill," he said, "I know it's risky to compare Ruth with Maris or Jimmy Brown with Red Grange because there are too many other factors involved, right?"

"Right," I said, feeling a little uneasy. Always watch out for people who start an argument by agreeing with you.

"But there's one sport where you can compare any athlete from any time or any place," he continued, "even the Greeks."

"Track and field?" I said. That bit about the Greeks had tipped it off.

"Right," he said, a little less enthusiastically. "I mean, the 40 miles they ran way back in the year one are the same 40 miles they run today, aren't they? Forty miles is 40 miles! And a modern runner can do it in about half the time!"

I was about to say something about their not having stop watches and record books back in the year one, but thought better of it, because the guy had a point.

"Every known record in track and field has been broken in the last ten or fifteen years, hasn't it?" he demanded. I had to agree. "And if these guys today are so superior to the ones thirty or forty years ago, why can't we assume that the athletes in other sports are superior too?"

It was a good argument and I had to agree in spite of myself, for lying in front of me on my desk was a news item: RYUN SETS RECORD FOR MILE AT 3:51.3. Fifteen years ago if anyone had told me that it was possible for a human being to run a 3:51 mile I would have told him he was out of his mind!

Obviously, something has happened. But what? Has the human organism grown stronger? Have training methods improved so much? Is there more dedication to a sport that has never returned much fame or fortune to its greatest performers?

I think the answer is a combination of all of these things. You don't have to be too astute to realize that people are getting bigger and stronger; you just have to look at your own or your neighbors' kids—and your gro-

213

cery bill! A high standard of living doesn't necessarily make all of us overweight and clogged with cholesterol, you know. It can make a heck of a lot of us bigger and stronger and healthier than any group of people the world has ever known.

And then there's the matter of training. There's absolutely no doubt about the fact that training methods have revolutionized track and field events. In the old days you just got out there and ran or jumped or threw. There was little planning and hardly any strategy to speak of. Now just about every race is laid out as carefully as a military maneuver. Look at the way Ryun ran his record race: the first quarter in 57.7 seconds, the half mile in 1:55.4 and the three-quarters in 2:55. Before the race Ryun had said that the ideal pace would be a 58-second first quarter, followed by two 59-second laps, passing the half-mile in 1:57 and the three-quarters in 2:56. "With a pace like that, I'm sure someone could run 3:52 or faster," he said.

As to the matter of dedication, I don't mean to take anything away from the great stars of thirty or forty years ago, but I must say that it seems to me that the track stars of today are dedicated to their sport as no other athletes in my memory. Take Ryun again. He comes from a comfortable middle-class home, he's well educated, he can be anything he wants to be, and yet here he is getting up at dawn and running about a hundred miles a week—and for what? A trip to Mexico City in 1968? He could go there on vacation. For fame and fortune? He could get a lot more by becoming a dentist, and work a lot less harder. For immortality? The type in that record book is awfully small, and he should know as well as anybody that his record will be broken in no time at all. No, it must be something else that drives Ryun and other young kids like him to battle that relentless second hand. If you have it, you don't wonder about it, and if you don't . . . well, you're just not a great athlete. You're a spectator, like me.

To get back to the matter at hand, the kids of today may seem like a bunch of supermen when compared with the old-timers, but they still have a long way to go to outdo some of the individual performances of the past.

Who turned in the greatest performance in track history?

It is generally conceded that Jesse Owens turned the trick at the Big Ten Championships in Ann Arbor, Michigan, on May 25, 1935, when he set four world records in one day. Jesse ran the 220-yard dash in 20.3 seconds, breaking the world record by 0.3; he knocked 0.4 off the 220-yard low hurdles record with a 22.6 clocking; he broke the broad jump record by 6⅛ inches with a leap of 26–8¼; and he tied the 100-yard dash record of 9.4!

In 1936, Jesse set a new world record for 100-meters, (10.2), and ran on the American team that set a world record of 39.8 for the 400-meter relay in the Olympic finals. Only three men ever defeated Jesse Owens in a sprint race—Ralph Metcalfe, Eulace Peacock, and James Johnson.

In a world-wide poll of sports experts, Jesse Owens was voted "Athlete of the Half-Century" for the years 1900–1950. He ended his career by turning professional to run on foot against race horses, which gives you a good idea of the professional possibilities open to track stars.

Another great Negro sprinter, Bob Hayes, ended his career by signing a professional football contract. In 60 races at 100 yards and 100 meters, including five 9.1 clockings at 100 yards, Hayes lost only twice.

Who were the only two men ever to beat Bob Hayes?

They were Harry Jerome, Canada's greatest sprinter, and Roger Sayers, whose brother Gale joined Hayes as a National Football League rookie sensation in 1965. Incidentally, after losing to Jerome and Sayers in the same week in 1962, Hayes ran up a string of 44 straight victories (including the Olympic 100 meters) before turning pro.

Another Olympic 100 meters champion had a streak almost twice as long as Hayes' . . . but not in the sprints. This great hurdler, whose boyhood idol was Jesse Owens, won 82 consecutive races, indoors and out, a feat doubly remarkable because of the ever-present danger of hitting a hurdle and losing stride; there aren't many winning streaks in the hurdles.

What great hurdler was also an Olympic 100-meter champion?

His name was Harrison Dillard, and he ran the Olympic sprint instead of the hurdles because in the USA's 1948 Olympic trials he hit several hurdles and could not finish the race. Dillard showed he was a real champion by coming back to make the team in the 100 meters, and then winning at the London Olympics. Four years later, "Bones" came out of retirement to win the Olympic high hurdles title at Helsinki.

Because the high hurdles are 3 feet, 6 inches high, tall hurdlers have an advantage over short ones, 5'–10" being considered the minimum height for a good hurdler. Yet one 5'–10" hurdler was as good as they come, winning nine National AAU high hurdles championships, and carving out his own unbeaten streak of 55 victories in indoor races from 1960 through 1964.

Who was the short high hurdler who won the 1964 Olympic gold medal in his event?

Hayes Jones. Jones, who used great speed and perfect hurdling form to overcome his lack of height, really "owned" the indoor hurdles. In fact, when he retired he held the meet record in his event in every one of the 18 major indoor meets. Although he never held the outdoor world record, Jones went on to win the 1964 Olympic gold medal in the high hurdles.

217

You might think that the female Jesse Owens would be Wilma Rudolph, but you'd be wrong. At one time, in 1948, a Dutch housewife held seven world records at once, including the 100 yards, 100 meters, high jump, broad jump and 80-meters hurdles.

Who was the woman track star who held seven world records at once?

She was Francina ("Fanny") Blankers-Koen, and although she was 30 years old in 1948, she went on to produce *two more* world records. At age 32, Fanny set a new standard for the 220-yard dash, and at 33 she proved she was still the world's most versatile trackswoman by setting a new world record in the pentathlon, raising the mark by an amazing 771 points to 4692 points. That's like knocking 20 seconds off the mile record!

Of all running events, the mile seems to be the most fascinating to the fans. And Kansas seems to be the place where great milers grow best in the United States. In fact, four Kansas milers have become world record holders.

How many Kansans have held world records in the middle distances?

Glenn Cunningham, Archie San Romani, Wes Santee and, of course, Jim Ryun. But at the time this book was written, only Cunningham and Ryun ever held the mile record. San Romani's record was for 2,000 meters and Santee's for 1,500 meters (the "Metric Mile"). Ryun also holds the record at 880 yards. Cunningham set his mile record, 4:06.8, in 1934. He actually ran a 4:04.4 mile indoors, but it was paced by a quartet of quarter-milers and was never accepted as a record.

Who has run more under-four-minutes miles than anyone else?

Peter Snell of New Zealand broke four minutes 15 times, but Herb Elliott of Australia did it *17* times! Even more remarkable, Elliott, although he scorned weak opposition and constantly raced against the best runners in the world, never lost a mile or 1,500 meters race.

Many track fans feel that a strong finishing kick is the secret of success in the mile. "Give me a miler who can sprint," they say, "and he'll come from behind to win in the homestretch."

How important is a big "kick" to a miler?

Not nearly as important as most people think. Cordner Nelson, editor of *Track & Field News*, recently analyzed 89 important mile and 1,500 meter races to find out. He discovered that the leader coming into the homestretch won 82 per cent of those races. Running is just like every other human activity . . . you can't afford to leave everything till the last minute.

How many men have held seven or more world records at one time?

Four: Paavo Nurmi of Finland, Gunder Hagg of Sweden, Emil Zatopek of Czechoslovakia, and Ron Clarke of Australia—all distance runners. Nurmi set his records from 1922 through 1931, Hagg ruled the roost in the Forties until he was declared a professional in 1945, Zatopek, a Czech army officer, was supreme in the Fifties, and Clarke is still running today.

Historically, Americans have been inferior distance runners. In fact, only four Americans have ever held world records at distances of two miles or over. Three of them should be easy to remember . . . but you have to be a real expert to be able to name them all.

Which four American runners have held world records at two miles or over?

Most sports fans know that Bob Schul held the two-mile record in 1964–65, and that Billy Mills and Gerry Lindgren ran a near dead-heat as both set a new six-mile record in 1965. The hard one is Don Lash, the great Indiana distance man of the middle 1930's. Lash, running in the Princeton Invitational in 1936, became the first American ever to hold a world record at a distance longer than a mile, breaking Nurmi's mark of 8:59.6 with an 8:58.4 performance. Three and a half months later, Hockert, another Finn, took Lash's record away from him by running 8:57.4.

Long before the fiberglass pole made 16- and 17-foot pole vaults commonplace, Cornelius Warmerdam startled the world with the first 15-foot clearance. In fact, between 1940 and 1944, "Dutch" Warmerdam bettered 15 feet outdoors 43 times! It wasn't until seven years later that anyone else vaulted 15 feet outdoors, and then, strangely, two men did it on the same day.

HOW FAST AND HOW HIGH CAN THEY GO?

Which two pole vaulters cleared 15 feet on the same day?

Don Cooper of Nebraska and Don Laz of Illinois became history's second and third 15-footers on April 21, 1951. Bob Richards, the "Vaulting Vicar" who had already cleared the height in indoor meets that winter, didn't join Cooper and Laz with an outdoor clearance until three weeks later, on May 11.

Warmerdam used a bamboo pole; Richards and Don Bragg used a steel pole; and although fiberglass poles were being used as early as 1952 (by decathlon man Bob Mathias), the "glass" pole didn't become popular until lesser-known vaulters catapulted to 16-foot vaults using it. John Uelses made the first 16-foot vault in 1962, and John Pennel first cleared 17 feet a year later.

How much extra height does the fiberglass pole provide?

Experts estimate that the fiberglass pole can add nearly two feet to a vaulter's efforts, but they hasten to add that the gymnastics involved in mastering fiberglass technique are far more difficult than vaulting with a bamboo or a metal pole.

Some athletes prefer to do their jumping without a pole, but not all of them disdain using equipment that might help them a bit.

After Charley Dumas set a world record by high jumping 7 feet, ½ inch, John Thomas and Valery Brumel later raised the mark to almost unbelievable heights. But between Dumas and Thomas, another Russian, Yuri Stepanov, became the first non-American in history to

hold the high jump record. A storm of controversy raged around his record.

Why was Yuri Stepanov's high-jump record called into question?

When Yuri Stepanov bettered Dumas' record with a 7'1" jump in Moscow in 1957, he wore a special shoe with a built-up sole approximately an inch thick. The German press dubbed it the "Catapult-shoe," and the International Amateur Athletic Federation withheld recognition of the record for more than a year while debating if use of the shoe was unfair. Finally, the IAAF accepted the record as valid, and then immediately contradicted itself by banning the shoe.

Thomas and Brumel staged a series of epic stratospheric battles, with the Russian winning all but one of them. But their friendly two-man feud ended when Brumel retired after being injured in a Moscow scooter accident.

What were John Thomas' and Valeriy Brumel's highest jumps?

Thomas' best was 7'3¾", a world record when he cleared it at the 1960 Olympic trials. Brumel improved the record to 7'4", then 7'4½" in 1961, cleared 7'5" and 7'5½" in 1962, and finally reached 7'5¾" at the 1963 USA–Russian meet at Moscow in 1963.

Another classic two-man rivalry between an American and a Russian has been staged in the broad jump between Ralph Boston and Igor Ter-Ovanesyan. Ralph and "Ter" have become good friends over the years, but Igor has never won from Boston outdoors. Besides Boston, only three other men have beaten Ter-Ovanesyan since 1958— the Americans Ernie Shelby and Bo Roberson, and Lynn Davies of Great Britain. The only man to beat Boston outdoors was another Russian, little-known Leonid Barkovsky, who topped Boston by a quarter of an inch in the USA–Russian meet in 1964, 26'4¼" to 26'4".

Most world records are the result of keen competition.

But Parry O'Brien was so much better than his fellow shot-putters that over the years 1952–58 he lost only three times in nearly 200 meets. Yet Parry broke the world record in the shot *16* times, improving it from 58–10½ to 63–4 in seven years.

In what year did Parry O'Brien retire from the shot put?

He hasn't retired yet—not through 1966, at least. In fact, at age 34, the durable O'Brien, now a bank vice-president, was still getting better. In May, 1966, Parry won 14 indoor and outdoor national championships in the shot put, and he developed a new style of putting which revolutionized the event.

In 1965, Randy Matson became the new king of the shot put with a heave of 70'7¼" inches while a sophomore at Texas A&M. Between O'Brien and Matson, though, a couple of pretty fair shot-putters held the coveted world record.

Who held the shot-put record between 1960 and 1965?

Bill Neider broke O'Brien's record in 1960 with a mark of 65'10", and Dallas Long eventually raised the record to 67'10" in 1964 before Matson took over. Neider was the 1960 Olympic champion at Rome, and Long won the Olympic title at Tokyo in 1964.

In the first USA–Russian meet, Rafer Johnson took the world decathlon record away from Vasily Kuznetsov of the Soviets. Although Kuznetsov regained the record in May, 1960, Johnson recaptured it in July and went on to win the Olympic decathlon in September from C. K. Yang and Kuznetsov. Johnson was almost unbeatable, but he did lose once.

Who was the only man to defeat Rafer Johnson?

Milt Campbell of Plainfield, New Jersey, and Indiana University was the only man to defeat Rafer Johnson in a decathlon. Big Milt scored when it counted, too, winning the gold medal at Melbourne in the 1956 Olympics. Johnson was second, with Kuznetsov, as usual, close behind.

The word "decathlon" comes from the Greek words *deca*, ten, and *athlon*, a contest. In modern track and field, it consists of ten events, contested over a two-day program.

What are the ten events of the decathlon?

First day: 100-meter dash, broad jump, shot put, high jump, 440-yard run. Second day: 110-meter high hurdles, discus throw, pole vault, javelin throw, and 1,500-meter run.

One woman in track history was as versatile as Rafer Johnson. In the 1932 Women's AAU meet, this Texas girl, competing as a one-woman team, won five national championships plus the team title. At one time or another, she set world records in the hurdles, the high jump and the javelin, and later became the greatest woman golfer of her time.

Who was America's greatest woman athlete?

She was Mildred "Babe" Didrickson. On that memorable day in 1932 the 18-year-old Babe scored 30 points all by herself, while the runner-up team of more than 20 women from the Illinois AC scored only 22 points. Besides winning five events outright, Babe also tied for first in the high jump—with a new world record of 5′3¾₁₆″!

World records are made to be broken, they say, but one world record lasted 25 years, the most durable track and field mark ever set.

What was the most durable track and field record ever set?

It was Jesse Owens' broad jump record of 26–8¼, set on May 25, 1935. And it wasn't until August 12, 1960 that Jesse's mark was broken. On that day, Ralph Boston jumped 26–11¼. A month later, Boston erased Owens' 24-year-old Olympic record of 26–5⅜ with a leap of 26–7⅞.

Maybe the fact that the most durable track record lasted only 25 years is the answer to the question put to me at the beginning of this chapter. It's been well over 34 years since Babe Ruth retired, and it's going to be quite a few years more before anyone breaks his home run record. It's been over 25 years since Joe DiMaggio hit in 56 consecutive games, and the possibility that that record will ever be broken hasn't even been suggested.

I may be wrong, but it seems to me that track and field records will continue to fall because all it takes to break them are dedication, training, and will. I haven't noticed that the young baseball, football, and basketball players of today are lacking in either dedication or willingness to train. What they may be lacking in is the will to break records—and rightly so. What they should have more than anything else is the will to *win*, not the will to break records. If they do set new records, those records are no more than a by-product of their will to win, and are usually due more to luck than to dedication.

In the final analysis, I'd say that the reason track and field athletes continue to set new records is that their sport depends very little on luck. They battle continually against the clock and the tape measure . . . and the clock and the tape measure seldom make mistakes or have bad days or play above their heads.

13

Court Royalty

Is it true that they don't allow a doctor to practice on his own family? I really don't know . . . seems to me I saw a movie once on that theme. Anyway, what I'm getting at is that basketball to me is something like my own family: it's one of the toughest things for me to be objective about. For the longest time I broadcast the games of the Buffalo area teams—Canisius, Niagara, St. Bonaventure, and the University of Buffalo. I'm shaking my head as I write this, because some of my experiences still seem unbelievable. Like the time I was broadcasting the Canisius-St. Bonaventure game and some of the Bonnie rooters started heckling me. My mother, who was sitting near them, went after them with her pocketbook. I couldn't do a thing. I was too busy broadcasting.

Then there was the time the University of Buffalo played Buffalo State Teachers at the State Teachers gym and I wasn't allowed in. There was a broadcast of the game that night, but not from WGR. Don't ask me why they wouldn't let me in, they just wouldn't. But there were plenty of broadcasts of other great games. Like the Canisius four-overtimes win over North Carolina State in the N.C.A.A. regionals at Madison Square Garden when a kid named Frannie Corcoran hit a jumper with the gun going off, or the night Hank Nowak stuffed Hot Rod Hundley, or any night Canisius played Niagara. When I think of the great players I've watched, the Al Butlers, the Tom Stiths, the Fred Crawfords, the Zeke Sinicolas, the Larry Costellos, I still get goose pimples. Like the way you probably get when you think of all the great games played in your area. And each area *does* have its great ones—at the Garden in New York, the Palestra in Philly, the Cow Palace in San Francisco, and the palaces everywhere that have produced court royalty.

It has been said that the game of basketball is America's one great contribution to the world of sports. The game is typically American in that it was invented out of whole cloth, so to speak: someone was given a problem, he analyzed it, considered the alternatives, and came up with a solution. It sounds simple, but what would *you* do if someone ordered you to invent a new team game?

How and why was basketball invented?

During the summer of 1890, the need for some new game became imperative at Springfield College (known then as the International Y.M.C.A. Training School) in Springfield, Massachusetts. Young coaches and athletic directors had gathered there from many different states for the summer term and all expressed complaints about the lack of interest in their winter gymnasium classes. There was little interest in the type of work that had been

introduced by R. J. Roberts, a one-time circus performer who had inaugurated a system of exercises that he had termed body-building work.

The directors of the school agreed that what was needed was an indoor team sport that could compete successfully with football and baseball, which were largely responsible for the Y.M.C.A.'s high summer and fall recruitment of members.

They turned the whole problem over to Dr. James Naismith, a Canadian instructor at the school, and they couldn't have picked a better man. Dr. Naismith was the type who went about things methodically. First, he examined all outdoor team sports, and noticed that the one thing most of them had in common was that they used a ball, which was driven, thrown, or struck toward a goal. All right, he'd start with a ball, but since the game he was seeking would have to be played indoors, it could not be small and hard like a baseball, since an uncontrolled baseball would be dangerous indoors.

Second, he noticed that the most popular team sports featured body contact and hard running, both of which would be dangerous in a small area with hard floors. His game would have to be slowed down somehow, with no free, hard running and a minimum of body contact. Along with this he noticed that the roughest play occurred when one team was near another's goal.

His solutions to these problems? First, use a large, lightweight ball, like a soccer ball, which could be easily controlled and wouldn't damage the players or the premises if it did get out of control. Second, make it illegal to run with the ball (have the man in possession bounce it along, or something like that) or to gain possession by wresting it from an opponent by brute force. As for the rough play around the goals, eliminate it by placing the goals over the players' heads. (Who could get hurt jumping up and down under a goal?)

Sometime in the winter of 1890–1891, Dr. Naismith nailed up two peach baskets at opposite ends of the gymnasium, chose up sides, threw in a soccer ball, and basketball was born!

THEY'LL NEVER MAKE IT... THEY'LL NEVER MAKE IT....

How did the dribble come into being?

The dribble was originally a defensive measure. When a player had possession of the ball and was so closely guarded that he could not pass it to one of his teammates, the only thing that he could do was to lose possession of

232

the ball voluntarily in such a way that he might possibly recover it.

He accomplished this by rolling or bouncing the ball on the floor. In a short time players realized that by bouncing the ball rapidly they could control it as well.

During the Christmas vacation of 1891 a number of Springfield College students went home and some of them started the game in their local Y.M.C.A.'s. There were no printed rules at the time and each student brought back his own version of the game.

It wasn't until January, 1892, that the school paper first put the rules of the game in print under the heading, "A New Game."

The first set of printed rules signalled the rapid spread of basketball to all parts of the United States and throughout Europe and South America. Soldiers introduced basketball in the Philippines in 1900 and the army of occupation taught the game to the Germans during World War I.

However, it wasn't until 1936 that basketball got its biggest boost when it was included in the Olympic Games at Berlin. Basketball had finally arrived as a major sport.

From then on basketball—scholastic, collegiate and professional—grew even quicker than the famed "Topsy" from *Uncle Tom's Cabin.*

One of the biggest boons to basketball's popularity was the staging of well-attended doubleheaders at New York City's Madison Square Garden. These games more than any one single thing placed basketball in the big-time. In addition, the intersectional games played at the Garden were of paramount importance in standardizing rule interpretations and introducing all styles of play to all parts of the nation.

The start of college basketball at Madison Square Garden was on December 29, 1934. Ask any basketball fan which teams played in that opening doubleheader and they will always recall two of them.

Which two teams initiated basketball's first great rivalry?

They were N.Y.U. and Notre Dame and the meeting between these two teams became one of college basketball's greatest rivalries. The other two teams on that opening night were Westminster and St. John's. N.Y.U. beat Notre Dame, 25–18, and Westminster defeated St. John's, 37–33.

Two post-season national tournaments, the National Collegiate Athletic Association and the National Invitation (held annually in Madison Square Garden) have also done much for the game. The N.I.T. was started in 1938 by the Metropolitan Basketball Writers Association and the N.C.A.A. began a year later.

There was a time when teams were permitted to play in both post-season tournaments. Only one college has ever won both.

Which is the only college team to have won both the N.I.T. and the N.C.A.A. tournaments?

In 1950, Nat Holman, the City College (C.C.N.Y.) basketball coach molded a team of five starters, four of whom were sophomores, into the nation's best. The Beavers won both competitions. The team was composed of Irwin Dambrot, a senior, and sophomores Al Roth, Eddie

Warner, Eddie Roman and Floyd Lane. Norman Mager alternated as a starter.

Long before Holman gained his fame as the City College basketball coach, he played on a team in the 1920's, a time known as the "golden era of sports."

Which team is considered the most famous in the history of basketball?

No basketball history is complete without mention of the Original Celtics. Often considered the greatest team to race up and down the court, they took on all comers in an annual 150-game schedule, usually winning 135 games or so. The scoring stars were Nat Holman and Johnny Beckman. Either Horse Haggerty or Joe Lapchick, who went on to coach St. John's University and the New York Knickerbockers, played center and Chris Leonard and Dutch Dehnert were the guards.

How many times has an undefeated team gone on to win the N.C.A.A. tournament?

Only three times in the history of college basketball has a team gone undefeated for an entire season and then won the National Collegiate Athletic Association championship tournament.

The University of San Francisco did it in 1956 with Bill Russell and K. C. Jones. Incidentally, when Russell arrived at San Francisco from McClymonds High (also in San Francisco) the college didn't even have a gymnasium. The team was known as the "Homeless Dons." By the time Russell left, he had led the Dons to two straight N.C.A.A. Championships and 45 successive victories.

In 1957, the University of North Carolina accomplished the feat with Lenny Rosenbluth the standout, and, finally, in 1964, it was the University of California at Los Angeles.

U.C.L.A. didn't figure in preseason ratings. The favorites on the national scene were Loyola of Chicago, with a seasoned team, and New York University. But out of the pack came U.C.L.A., coached by Johnny Wooden. The

Bruins averaged 88.9 points per game and exercised superior ball control with Walt Hazzard and Gail Goodrich, a pair of prized backcourt men. Keith Erickson, Jack Hirsh, Ken Washington and Frank Slaughter made up the rest of the team. Coach Johnny Wooden alternated his starters.

Pro basketball teams have bettered the 150-point mark per game and collegiate and schoolboy teams are not far behind in point production. This rash of scoring is comparatively new to basketball. There were days three and four decades ago when, for example, City College edged Villanova, 11–9, or lost to Carnegie Tech, 13–12.

One player more than anyone else is credited with starting the basketball scoring revolution.

Which player started the basketball scoring revolution?

Angelo Enrico ("Hank") Luisetti, born January 16, 1916, in the Telegraph Hill section of San Francisco, the same area which provided the New York Yankees with Joe DiMaggio, Frank Crosetti and Tony Lazzeri, is credited with giving basketball the same prominence Babe Ruth gave baseball and Red Grange football.

Luisetti made the one-handed shot famous and basketball has never been the same since. Luisetti amazed the basketball world when he scored 305 points in 18 games and 70 points in a two-game weekend series in his freshman year at Stanford.

Luisetti was but a boy when he began shooting baskets. He developed his feathery one-handed shot at Galileo High School in San Francisco and perfected it in college. Thus, a college kid with a "crazy" shot changed basketball forever.

FOUL, FOUL !

Pro basketball in its past 20 years of existence has had three standout "big" men. Can you name the first of the basketball giants? He attended DePaul University and originally planned to study for the priesthood.

COURT ROYALTY

Who was basketball's first "big" man?

George Mikan, 6'10", 250 lbs., was the first of the big men. He had a tremendous influence on the game, first in college, where he was an All-American in 1944, 1945 and 1946, and then with the Minneapolis Lakers (now the Los Angeles Lakers). His play had much to do with moving the National Basketball Association from its floundering infancy to stabilized maturity.

He spent 10 years with the Lakers and was the first player to reach the 10,000-point scoring plateau. He left basketball with 11,764 points to his credit after having led Minneapolis to six N.B.A. titles in his first seven seasons with the club.

Basketball was so grateful for his coming that when a flock of historians sat down to select the basketball player of the first half-century, few dissented at the nomination of George Mikan.

Mikan didn't give the appearance of a basketball player. He started in an era where the sport wasn't ready for a man of his size.

Mikan retired from the game as "Mr. Basketball" in 1956. He coached the Lakers for one year in 1957. It was in the NBA season of 1956–1957 that another "giant" stepped in. This one they called "Mr. Defense" and he started the Boston Celtics on an unprecedented dynasty.

Which "big" man is known as "Mr. Defense"?

Bill Russell. Bill has often been referred to as the Albert Einstein of basketball—not in intellect, but in his effect on the sport. No individual has had more influence on a trend

ACTUALLY, I FEEL SORTA...

... GUILTY 'BOUT PLAYIN' THIS GAME!

of play in basketball since Hank Luisetti made his one-hand shot popular.

Russell called attention to some different aspects of the game—rebounding and jumping. They had been fundamental parts of the game from basketball's inception but Bill found a new way to apply them.

Russell's technique of blocking shots soon gave him the title of "Mr. Defense." He also triggered the fast break. He was a pioneer of many defensive basketball innovations.

What was the Boston Celtics' record in Russell's ten seasons with Boston?

Starting with 1956–1957, Boston has won the Eastern Division title every year until the Philadelphia 76ers snapped the string in 1965–1966.

In fact, the Celtics have lost only one N.B.A. title in Russell's time, to the St. Louis Hawks in 1957–1958.

Bill Russell, the pioneer of many defensive basketball innovations, embarked on a new career for the 1966–1967 season. After the retirement of Arnold ("Red") Auerbach, who parlayed a 20-year N.B.A. coaching career into 1,037 victories, Russell was named coach of the Boston Celtics —the first time a Negro has attained that position in a major sport.

In the 1959–1960 N.B.A. season the third giant who was to have a tremendous influence on basketball arrived on the scene.

Which of basketball's "big" men is known as "Mr. Offense"?

Wilt ("The Stilt") Chamberlain, 7'1", the greatest scorer the game has known thus far. On the night of November 16, 1962, Wilt rolled up 73 points against the New York Knickerbockers, the most points ever scored in

241

one game at Madison Square Garden. Some three months later, in Hershey, Pennsylvania, against the same Knicks, he poured in 100 points. That's an N.B.A. record, of course, but that's not all: he holds the scoring record in every basketball arena in which he has ever played an N.B.A. game!

No date in Wilt's basketball life is more important than February 14, 1966. It was in Charlestown, West Virginia, against the Detroit Pistons. Wilt scored 41 points that night, but the 38th point was the big one in his life. It gave the Philadelphia giant his 20,842nd point and established him as the greatest scorer in N.B.A. history.

Chamberlain's basketball success is like a dream come true for a youngster who grew to such a monstrous size that he was considered a freak. His father grumbled because he grew too quickly out of his clothes and even his bed.

Wilt had trouble playing with the neighborhood youngsters. There was no place for him in kid games. He was just too big and strong. When he was still a teen-ager at Overbook (Pa.) High School he was seven feet tall. Basketball had never seen such a size before so Wilt was molded into a player. He responded by smashing every conceivable scholastic record. At the same time he was lionized, sought-after, proselytized and exploited.

Chamberlain finally selected the University of Kansas and before he left it he smashed every possible record. About the only thing Wilt and his coach, Phog Allen, couldn't put together was a N.C.A.A. championship team.

By the time Chamberlain is ready to hang up his basketball sneakers a fourth giant should be ready for the pro ranks. He is Lew Alcindor, who broke every New York City basketball scoring record with 2,067 points and

2,022 rebounds, and gained nationwide publicity as colleges throughout the country sought his talents. Alcindor finally chose U.C.L.A. and, in his freshman year, made shambles of the yearling records.

Alcindor played for Power Memorial Academy, a Catholic school in New York City. Power, with Alcindor, ran up 71 straight victories and it sent record seekers scurrying to the books to find the longest scholastic winning streak.

Which team holds the longest scholastic winning streak?

Coach Ernie Blood's Passaic, New Jersey, Wonder Team ran up 159 consecutive victories before losing to Hackensack, New Jersey, 39–35, February 6, 1925. Incidentally, it was DeMatha High School of Hyattsville, Maryland, which stopped the Power streak.

Who held the N.B.A. scoring record before Wilt Chamberlain?

Bob Pettit, of the St. Louis Hawks. Pettit is another success story. He was a 6'9" center who came out of L.S.U. in 1954. He was a spindly one, too skinny for the pros they thought. But 30 pounds and 20,841 points later, they were convinced. Pettit used his one-handed jump shot to become the first player to reach the 20,000 point plateau. He never finished lower than fourth in N.B.A. scoring.

He led Baton Rouge High School to two state titles and then attended L.S.U. where in three seasons he scored 2,002 points and rewrote the Southeastern Conference basketball books.

The key to his success was a one-handed jump shot that

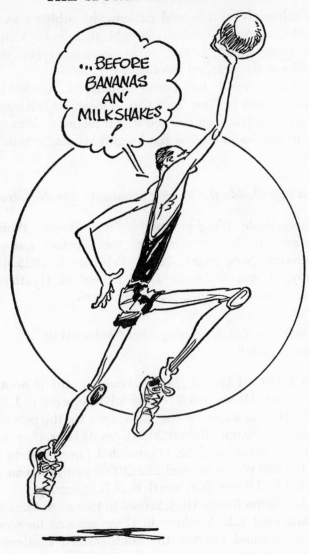

he fired from anywhere on the court the moment he had a teammate to screen for him.

All of basketball's superstars are not the "big" men. There is one relatively small player who seems to combine all the elements that make for the perfect basketball player.

Who is the perfect basketball player?

Since he donned a basketball uniform for the Crispus Attucks High School in Indianapolis, Oscar Robertson has played the game as though Dr. Naismith invented it for him alone. Coaches and players consistently agree that when the "Big O" does something, it's almost as if he was demonstrating at a basketball clinic, he executes plays and moves so perfectly.

Robertson is equipped with just about everything: sufficient size (6'5"), weight (215 lbs.), strength, speed, shooting touch, court sense, ball handling skill, passing ability, defensive toughness, remarkable stamina and alertness. In short, a coach's, owner's, and fan's dream.

In high school Robertson led a team that won 45 games in a row. It was the first time an Indianapolis school won the state championship and the first Negro school to perform the feat and repeat as champion.

More than 80 colleges from coast-to-coast clamored for his services. He picked the University of Cincinnati and led the Bearcats to 79 victories in 87 games. During his stay he established 13 N.C.A.A. records and the Bearcats drew 805,159 to their home games.

Jerry West is another relatively small man who has everything it takes to make a perfect basketball player. His "Wild West Shows" put the Mountaineers of West

Virginia University on the national basketball map. In **1960** he was the Los Angeles Lakers' first draft choice, **and** his drives through much taller men for his twisting layups and the seeming ease with which he launches his jump shots have made him one of the greatest scorers in basketball history.

When West came to the Lakers he joined another superstar and together they have become the most prolific scoring combination in the history of pro basketball.

What is the greatest scoring combination in the history of pro basketball?

Jerry West and Elgin Baylor, of the Los Angeles Lakers. Baylor learned his basketball in Washington, D. C. As a youngster he used to play by himself when no one was around and he perfected his style by weaving and bobbing against imaginary opponents. He originally entered the College of Idaho, but switched to Seattle University where he turned the Chieftains into a national power.

When Baylor graduated from Seattle the present Lakers were in Minneapolis and floundering. The season before, the Lakers won 19 and lost 53 and the customers stayed away in droves.

Elgin changed all that. In fact, he is credited with singlehandedly having saved a franchise.

In Baylor's first year he averaged 34.9 points per game (fourth highest in the league) and 1,050 rebounds (third in the league). The Lakers jumped from last place to second and beat St. Louis for the division title in the N.B.A. semi-finals. They finally lost to the Boston Celtics for the title.

Probably the most popular and greatest of all playmakers was once no more than a name on a slip of paper in a hat that the Boston Celtics didn't want. The name was Bob Cousy's.

How did Bob Cousy become a member of the Boston Celtics?

Cousy, the Houdini of the Hardwoods, starred at Holy Cross but when the time rolled around for the N.B.A. draft the Celtics passed him by. His 6'1½" in a game where 6'4" is considered "medium" and 6'8" "okay" scared the Celtics away.

Instead, Cousy was drafted by Tri-Cities, a team owned by Ben Kerner, who now owns the St. Louis Hawks. Kerner traded Cousy to the Chicago Stags, but before the season started the Stags folded and Cousy was one of the players who was up for grabs. Bob's name was in a hat with those of Max Zaslofsky and Andy Phillip. Cousy was the one the Celtics wanted the least and got. They were never sorry.

In his 13 seasons, Cousy scored 18,973 points, but perhaps more important were the 7,786 assists he made. In addition to the all-time National Basketball Association record for assists, Cousy achieved the following other distinctions—Most Valuable Player Award, 10 consecutive All-League selections, and membership on six championship teams.

On March 17, 1963, everybody at the Boston Garden was singing, "We love you Cooz." It was the end of the professional player career of Bob Cousy, the game's greatest magician of all time.

Who was the "Iron Man" of basketball?

Harry Gallatin, of the New York Knickerbockers. Up to his retirement in the spring of 1959, Gallatin had never

PLEASE, ANYBODY **BUT** COUSY...

missed a game from the time he had joined New York. He played 682 successive regular season games and 64 playoff contests, 746 games in all!

What was the lowest score in N.B.A. history?

The lowest score was registered in Minneapolis on November 22, 1950, when the Pistons (the present Detroit franchise) edged the Minneapolis Lakers, 19–18.

What is the all-time winning streak by an N.B.A. team?

Seventeen games in a row, set by the Washington Capitols in 1946. Boston duplicated the feat in 1959. Incidentally, both teams were coached by Red Auerbach.

How many rookies have scored over 2,000 points their first year?

Four. They were Wilt Chamberlain of Philadelphia (2,702), Walt Bellamy of New York (2,495), Oscar Robertson of Cincinnati (2,165) and Rick Barry of the San Francisco Warriors (2,059). Barry, who was the nation's leading collegiate scorer at the University of Miami, scored 57 points against the Knicks on December 14, 1965. Only one rookie has scored more points in a single game.

Which rookie holds the record for most points scored in a single game?

Wilt Chamberlain, who hit 58 points twice in the 1959–1960 season when he broke in with the Philadelphia Warriors.

14

The Icemen Cometh

HOCKEY's a sport you might say I got through osmosis—
that is, by hearing about it constantly from my Canadian
cousin. I suppose that just about every family has a Canadian branch, and mine was no exception. That my cousin
came from Saskatoon, Saskatchewan, and had grown up
with Bill and Bun Cook made him about as tolerable as
male cousins can be, but he had to make things worse with
his constant assertions of Canadian superiority. And not
just in hockey (there was no argument about that—there
just aren't enough American players), but in everything
else—food, talk, clothes, everything. Who knows, maybe
he was right. But he was still a cousin. . . .

On June 25, 1965, something happened that may go a
long way toward changing my cousin's opinion. It was a
day on which New Yorkers sweltered more than usual, and
if they had any thoughts about hockey at all, it was in
association with ice and cooler things to come.

At New York's Plaza Hotel, the august Board of Gov-

ernors of the National Hockey League made plans to expose millions of more Americans to names like Richard, Howe, Beliveau and Hull and terms like icing, blue line and high sticking. In recent years expansion has gripped professional sports—baseball, basketball and football. Now blessed with wealthy backers—and the hope of na-

252

tional television—hockey joined the sports expansion bandwagon and the six-city N.H.L. grew to 12.

Big-time professional hockey, hitherto confined to New York, Boston, Chicago, Detroit, Montreal and Toronto, voted St. Louis, Los Angeles, San Francisco, Minnesota, Philadelphia and Pittsburgh into the league. The six new league cities will make up a separate division of play, and will play an inter-locking schedule with the six established teams. Under the new setup, each club will play 74 games a season, 24 of which will be against teams from the other division (two home and two away against each club).

If there ever was a reason for American kids wanting to play ice hockey, they now had it, believe me. The American ownership would *have* to give impetus to hockey in the States, a need that has long been recognized. When I worked the televised Stanley Cup playoffs in 1966, I interviewed Jack Kent Cooke of Los Angeles, and he was pointed in his desire to get the American boy on skates and playing hockey.

When was the last time there was a change in the N.H.L. structure?

When the New York Americans pulled out in 1942 and it left the league with six clubs.

Hockey, as a major sport, has come a long way since the first formal game of ice hockey was played in 1855 in Kingston, Ontario, with teams composed of soldiers of the Royal Canadian Rifles. Today, Kingston is considered the official birthplace of the game.

From which other sport was the comparatively new game of ice hockey derived?

Field hockey is one of the oldest stick-and-ball games in history and ice hockey is a new version of it. The word hockey itself is believed to come from the French word *hocquet*—the curved shepherd's crook. The game was first played by the Greeks and passed on to the Romans, who gave it over to the British.

The development of the steel ice skate around 1885 gave impetus to the rise of ice hockey as a major organized sport.

THE ICEMEN COMETH

What was the origin of the Stanley Cup?

By 1893, there was so much ice hockey activity that Frederick Arthur, Lord Stanley of Preston and the son of the Earl of Derby, then Governor General of Canada, put the Stanley Cup into competition for the best amateur team in the sport.

Lord Stanley purchased the trophy for ten British pounds ($48.67 at the time). Since 1910, when the National Hockey Association took possession of the Stanley Cup, the trophy has been the symbol of professional hockey supremacy. It has been competed for only by the National Hockey League teams since 1926 and has been under the exclusive control of the N.H.L. since 1946. There have been alterations to the structure of the Cup totalling $6,000. In addition, engraving costs are approximately $150 per year, or a total of $7,500 for the names engraved on the trophy since 1913.

What was the origin of ice hockey in the United States?

In 1893, two Yale tennis champions, Malcolm G. Chace and Arthur E. Foote, started the sport on the New Haven campus. The game quickly spread throughout the nation and three years later the Amateur Hockey League was formed in New York and a league was started in Baltimore.

The rise of the professional game stimulated amateur interest and presently there are more than 300 teams, including many in the N.C.A.A., registered with the Amateur Hockey Association.

Ice hockey first became part of the Olympic schedule in

the 1929 games in Amsterdam. Canada because of its experience in the sport emerged with the gold medals in 1920, 1924, 1928 and 1932. Great Britain finally snapped the Canadian string at the 1936 Olympics in Berlin.

Three years before hockey was accepted at the Olympic Games, the National Hockey League was organized in Montreal. Delegates representing the Montreal Canadiens, Montreal Wanderers, Ottawa and Quebec were present. These teams, along with the Toronto Arenas were admitted into the league. The clubs played a 22-game schedule during the 1917–1918 season.

Which was the first United States club to compete in the N.H.L.?

The Boston Bruins became the first United States entry to join the league in 1924. Two years later three United States teams—New York Rangers, Chicago Black Hawks and Detroit Cougars—were admitted into the league.

To the uninitiated, hockey looks like a 60-minute free-for-all. However, a player can get away with just so much. There is a carefully devised system of penalties, and players are sent to the penalty box for bad behavior for varying degrees of time, depending on the infraction.

Hockey is possibly the only major sport that actually compels a team to lose a player for a given amount of time when the player is penalized.

Who holds the N.H.L. record for the most penalty minutes in a season?

The Detroit Red Wings' bad boy, Howie Young, spent the incredible total of 273 minutes in the penalty box during the 1962–1963 season. The time was equivalent to more than four full games of the 70-game schedule. It is even more significant when one realizes the average player spends only one third of a game on the ice—or 20 minutes. Young's time off, then, is actually equivalent to missing almost 14 full games.

While on the subject of hockey and its roughhouse

tactics, the name Eddie Shore, the boisterous Boston defenseman who turned to managing when he stopped playing, has become a legend.

Shore, sometimes known as the firebrand of the ice, was hockey's roughest, toughest and most colorful star of his day. He was also one of the first to be named to Hockey's Hall of Fame.

Shore played hockey like a man possessed. Entirely oblivious to pain and injury, he collected over the years the most extensive damage ever handed out to a hockey player. His body was a mass of scars that criss-crossed their way from head to foot. He suffered, at one time or another, a serious spinal injury, many broken bones, a

gashed head, and a fractured jaw, and by the time he retired, all his teeth had been knocked out. It has been reported it took 600 stitches to mend his gashes. In addition, his scalp carried 19 scars.

Besides the Stanley Cup, many other prizes have been associated with the sport.

What are ice hockey's other trophies?

His Royal Highness, the Prince of Wales, donated the Prince of Wales Trophy to the N.H.L. in 1924. From 1927–1928 to 1937–1938 the award was presented to the team finishing first in the American Division of the N.H.L. Since the 1938–1939 season, when the N.H.L. reverted to one division, it has been presented to the team winning the league championship.

The Hart Trophy is awarded to the player judged to be the most valuable to his team.

The Lady Byng Trophy is given to the player who has exhibited the best sportsmanship and gentlemanly conduct combined with a high standard of playing ability. Lady Byng, wife of Canada's Governor General at the time, presented the Lady Byng Trophy in 1925. After Frank Boucher of the New York Rangers won the award seven times in eight seasons, he was given the trophy to keep and Lady Byng replaced it with another.

The Calder Trophy went into competition for the 1936–1937 season. It was given by Frank Calder, president of the N.H.L., to the outstanding rookie of the season.

The Vezina Trophy is an annual award honoring the memory of George Vezina, an outstanding goalie with the

THE ICEMEN COMETH

Montreal Canadiens who collapsed during an N.H.L. game Nov. 28, 1925, and died of tuberculosis a few months later. It is presented to the goalkeeper or goalkeepers who have played a minimum of 25 games and allowed the opposition the least number of goals.

The Ross Trophy is an annual award to the player who leads the league in scoring.

The James Norris Memorial Trophy is the newest of the N.H.L. achievement awards for regular-season play. Its recipient is the defensive player who demonstrates throughout the season the greatest all-around ability in that position.

The Smythe Trophy is an annual award to the most valuable player for his team in the entire playoffs.

Like any sport, hockey has had its super greats, men like Lester Patrick, Maurice Richard, Gordie Howe and Bobby Hull.

Who was the original "Mr. Hockey"?

Man and boy, Lester Patrick spent more than 40 years in big-time hockey, as player, manager, coach and owner. He is often referred to as "Mr. Hockey."

Patrick revolutionized the game, won fame as the greatest defenseman of them all, and sparked teams to the world championships in Stanley Cup competition. As a player and manager, he figured in over 20 such Stanley Cup successes.

Probably his most unforgettable moment came in March 1928 when the Patrick-coached New York Rangers were playing the powerful Montreal Maroons for the Stanley Cup.

During the second game, a flying puck caromed off a

hockey stick and struck Lorne Chabot, the Ranger goalie, square in the eye. The Rangers didn't have a reserve goalie capable of handling the nets. So manager Patrick, silver-thatched and approaching 50 years of age, donned a Ranger uniform and took over the nets.

The Rangers had gone on the ice expecting to see their coach cut to pieces in the nets. Instead his example gave them new spirit and drive. With Patrick playing like a fiend behind them, the Rangers went on to win the game and also the Stanley Cup.

THE ICEMEN COMETH

Who was the most exciting hockey player ever?

For 18 N.H.L. seasons Joseph Henri Maurice Richard, alias "The Rocket," put on his 12 pounds of shin and shoulder pads, ankle length underwear, skates and stovepipe pants to maintain his position as the most exciting hockey player ever. He was a demi-god to his rabid French-Canadien followers. A king, the goal scoring nonpareil, the most dynamic and dramatic star in professional hockey.

Richard scored his final goal for the Montreal Canadiens in the 1960 Stanley Cup playoffs. It was his 82nd in Stanley Cup play, a record, and it raised his lifetime total to 626.

On November 9, 1952, when the Rocket tallied his 325th goal, he became the N.H.L.'s highest individual scorer in history and the puck was sent to Queen Elizabeth of England.

Richard had a fiery temper that caused many a rhubarb around the league. One of the penalties imposed on him caused one of the most famous, or infamous, incidents in the sport.

A stiff penalty inflicted on Richard prompted the infamous Montreal riot of March 17, 1955, wherein disgruntled worshipers pelted the league president with assorted rancid grocery articles, turned over streetcars and broke store windows. Only an impassioned plea by Richard himself on radio and TV quieted them.

Richard was one player who had disdain for defensive records. Among his scoring marks is one for most points in a game.

What is the record for most points scored in a hockey game?

With five goals and three assists on December 28, 1944, Richard set the mark of eight points in a game. The victims of his scoring splurge were the Detroit Red Wings in a game played in Montreal.

Bert Olmstead, also of the Montreal Canadiens, tied the mark with four goals and four assists against Chicago at the Montreal Forum ten years later.

THE ICEMEN COMETH

Who is hockey's greatest craftsman?

Gordie Howe, the Detroit Red Wings' right wing, whose sloped shoulders tend to minimize his six-foot, 200-pound frame, is hockey's supreme craftsman because he does more things better than anybody, and that means skate, shoot, fight, score goals and engineer them.

On November 27, 1965, Howe pushed the puck past the Montreal Canadiens' goalie and everything stopped. Gordie Howe, who already was the game's top scorer, reached a new scoring plateau—his 600th goal. The next day the puck was placed in a gold encasement and sent to the Hockey Hall of Fame in Toronto.

When the 1965–1966 hockey season was over Howe claimed a career total of 624 goals, nine first team All-Star berths, six Most Valuable Player Awards and the N.H.L.'s scoring lead six times.

Incidentally, Howe holds virtually every Detroit season scoring record except one.

What Detroit scoring record does Gordie Howe not hold?

Assists. Howe ranks second to Ted Lindsay, who picked up 55 assists twice—in the 1949–1950 and 1956–1957 seasons. Howe's best was 49 in 1960–1961.

Hockey likes to call itself the world's fastest sport. Some players approach speeds of 30 miles an hour even in the confined areas of the rink. But reflexes are as important as sheer speed when players are near the net.

THAT'LL COST YOU A SPEEDING TICKET!

Who holds the record for the fastest three goals in ice hockey history?

Bill Mosienko, of the Chicago Black Hawks, knocked in three goals in a 21-second span during the third period on March 23, 1952. He accomplished the feat against the Rangers in Madison Square Garden at 6 minutes 9 seconds, 6:20 and 6:30. The two fastest goals were scored four seconds apart by Nels Stewart of the Montreal Maroons on January 3, 1931 at Montreal. They came in the first period.

THE ICEMEN COMETH

No matter how great the feat by Mosienko, another Black Hawk has become known as hockey's home-run hitter.

Who is known as hockey's home-run hitter?

Bobby Hull, in 1966, surpassed 50 goals—hockey's seemingly impassable barrier. He has displayed three secret weapons that have skyrocketed him to among the sport's all-time greats. He can change speed on the ice better than any player in the league. He has superior strength, which coupled with the ability to change speed makes him a difficult target for body checking. And finally, he has remarkable fortitude. Most N.H.L. forwards spend more than half the game resting on the bench. Hull's average playing time has been as high as 40 minutes.

Incidentally, Hull's slap and wrist shots are reputed to be faster than any player in the league. A survey revealed that his slap shot, the sport's flashiest weapon, has been clocked at 95 miles per hour. The slap shot is launched in a fashion similar to that a golfer uses when hitting a three iron.

Which goalie holds the longest shutout string?

A shutout is a big accomplishment in hockey. Alex Connell of the Ottawa Senators, during the 1927–1928 season, went 446 minutes and nine seconds without being scored on. His string included six shutouts. In the modern era the record belongs to Bill Durnan of the 1948–1949 Montreal Canadiens who held the opposition at bay for 309 minutes and 21 seconds, scoring four shutouts.

Who is the youngest manager in the National Hockey League?

Emile ("Cat") Francis, who serves as both general manager and coach of the New York Rangers was born September 13, 1926. Despite his size (five-foot-six, 150 pounds), Francis had a 14-year career as a professional goaltender, including part of six seasons in the N.H.L. with the Chicago Black Hawks and New York Rangers.

THE ICEMEN COMETH

Who holds the record for the most consecutive
appearances in Stanley Cup play?

Bernie ("Boom Boom") Geoffrion, who played with the
Montreal Canadiens and is currently a member of the
New York Rangers, appeared in 14 post-season series from
1951 to 1964.

Hockey, like most sports is filled with famous nicknames.

What are the first names of Chico Maki, Muzz Patrick,
Tim Horton, Dit Clapper, Toe Blake and Gump
Worsely.

Ronald Maki, Murray Patrick, Aubrey Clapper, Myles
Horton, Hector Blake and Lorne Worsley.

15

Saturday Heroes

A LOT of people these days are talking about football taking the place of baseball as the national sport. What they mean by football is, of course, pro football, for the hard-hitting, lightning-fast game the pros play seems to have captured the interest of the public far more than the collegiate variety ever did. But the fact remains that for most of its history football has been a game played by amateurs, and that pro football would be virtually impossible without the large talent pool provided by the college teams.

Unlike baseball, whose rules and basic patterns are pretty much the same today as they were a few years after the turn of the century, football has been constantly evolving; in fact, it seems that the only things about it that haven't changed are the dimensions of the playing field. Let's consider some of the milestones in football's history and development:

Which teams played in the first college football game?

Princeton and Rutgers played in the first game at New Brunswick, New Jersey, on November 6, 1869. Rutgers won the game 6 goals to 4, and it all stemmed from a challenge. Intra-school teams were very popular and both the Tigers and Scarlet Knights boasted good teams. Rutgers challenged Princeton to a series of three games. The first was played according to Rutgers' rules and it was

271

decided that the team scoring the first six goals would be the winner. The second game was played at Princeton, under the Princeton rules, with the team getting the first eight goals declared the winner. Princeton won that one, but the third game, because no one could agree on the ground rules, was called off.

When was the forward pass first introduced to college football?

Historians have excavated an account of how the first forward pass came into being in a story of the Yale-Princeton game of November 30, 1876. The brief mention indicated that the ball was thrown forward after a player with possession had been tackled.

Another account of a game between the same rivals in 1883 indicated that the ball was thrown 25 feet after it was snapped from center. Thus perhaps grew the concept of the modern forward pass.

The next incident of a forward pass took place in a Georgia-North Carolina game in 1895. The Carolina fullback got the ball and was undecided what to do with it. The Georgia players expected a kick and rushed the fullback, who had instructions to get rid of the ball fast as far down field as possible. He took a few steps to one side and threw a short distance forward to one of the players who went 70 yards for a touchdown.

Whenever the first forward pass was thrown it was obviously a long time ago and when and how it happened is an academic question. The passing attack as we know it today was perfected by two men Charley ("Gus") Dorais, the passer, and Knute Rockne, the No. 1 receiver, on the 1912–1913 Notre Dame teams.

In 1913 against Army at West Point they introduced the passing attack to the East. Dorais threw 21 passes and completed 17 for 243 yards. The wide-open style of attack, which gained big yardage, baffled the Cadets who had expected an old-fashioned, line-smashing game. The Irish won, 35–13, with all five touchdowns being set up or scored on passes.

Who developed the modern T-formation?

Clark Shaughnessy, of the University of Chicago, is the coach who is generally credited with developing the next great innovation in football—the modern T-formation.

The T-formation shifted the emphasis of the game from the running halfbacks to the passing quarterback, and part of its success and ready acceptance by even the most conservative coaches in the country was due to the stylish ball handling of a famous college quarterback.

Who was the first famous T-formation quarterback?

He was Frankie Albert, the star of Stanford's unbeaten Rose Bown team of 1940, who is ranked as one of the greatest exponent of the T the game has known, and that's saying something when you consider the great quarterbacks that have come and gone since then.

The 1940 Stanford team won 10 games in a row, scoring 196 points against 85 for its rivals, and then went on to whip Nebraska, 21–13, in the Rose Bowl. The remarkable thing about this team was that in 1939 Stanford had produced its worst record, winning only once, losing seven times and gaining one tie. But a new coach, a master at teaching the T-formation, took over in 1940. He was Clark

Shaughnessy, a fugitive from the University of Chicago, which had just de-emphasized sports to the extent of abolishing football.

Albert, as good as he was, had a tremendous group of backs to work with in Hugh Gallarneau, Pete Kmetovic and Norm Standlee. Many experts rank this backfield as one of the greatest of all time, worthy to be compared with the Army's 1944–1946 backfields and with Notre Dame's "Four Horsemen."

That Army backfield was a thing of beauty to watch, and the fact that it performed during wartime does not lessen the experts' enthusiasm.

Who were the stars of the 1944–1946 Army backfields?

Felix ("Doc") Blanchard, the fullback, and Glenn Davis, the halfback, helped the Cadets run roughshod over opponents for three years.

In 1944, the Cadets went undefeated in nine games, scoring the astounding total of 504 points against only 35. Entering their last college game against Navy in 1946, Blanchard, whose power enabled him to carry would-be tacklers along with him, and Davis, a swift, cagey runner, had engineered the Army teams to a three-year record of 26 victories and a tie—against Notre Dame. They became known as the "Touchdown Twins," with Blanchard as "Mr. Inside" and Davis as "Mr. Outside" for obvious reasons—Blanchard's power up the middle and Davis's swift jaunts around the ends.

While these two dominated the publicity that fell to the Army teams under Coach Earl ("Red") Blaik, there were two starting quarterbacks who called the plays that sent the Touchdown Twins on their way to glory.

The 1944 team was quarterbacked by Doug Kenna, who also gained All-America honors with Blanchard and Davis, and an alternate, Tom Lombardo, the team captain. But in 1945 and 1946, the signal-calling fell to a great tactician and fine passer, Arnold Tucker, who with Blanchard and Davis, one expert wrote, formed "probably the greatest backfield triumvirate in modern times. . . ."

Unfortunately Army's fourth backfield spot, while capably filled by Herschel Fuson and others, never really received "fourth horseman" status.

We have been using as a standard the backfield of the 1924 Notre Dame team—the celebrated "Four Horsemen," probably the greatest backfield ever put together. Knute Rockne's team that year went through 10 games undefeated, scoring 285 points to its opponents' 54.

Who were the "Four Horsemen"?

The quarterback was Harry Stuhldreher, the halfbacks were Jim Crowley and Don Miller and the fullback was Elmer Layden. Crowley and Layden later became successful coaches—Sleepy Jim at Fordam and Layden at his alma mater.

These four amazing football players comprised one of the swiftest and lightest backfields that ever hit the gridiron. They averaged only 157 pounds, extremely light for major college football but the essential factor in their success. They were like horses who could canter, trot and gallop. Layden was the heaviest at 164 pounds, Stuhldreher the lightest at 154, with Miller and Crowley somewhere in between.

How did the phrase "Four Horsemen" originate?

Grantland Rice, one of the most famous sports writers ever to lug his typewriter up to a press box, coined the phrase in 1924 when Notre Dame defeated Army, 13–7, before 55,000 spectators at the Polo Grounds in New York.

What Rice wrote in his lead has become sports-writing literature—words many present-day sports writers wished they had written. This was Rice's lead paragraph:

"Outlined against a blue-gray October sky, the Four Horsemen rode again. In dramatic lore they are known as Famine, Pestilence, Destruction and Death. These are only aliases. Their real names are Stuhldreher, Miller,

Crowley and Layden. They formed the crest of the South Bend cyclone before which another fighting Army football team was swept over the precipice at the Polo Grounds yesterday afternoon as 55,000 spectators peered down on the bewildering panorama spread on the green plain below." They just don't write 'em like that anymore.

Rice later wrote that the seed for the idea had been planted in his mind a year earlier when Army met Notre Dame in Ebbets Field in Brooklyn because the World Series between the Giants and the Yankees was being played at Coogan's Bluff. Rice chose to report on the football game. He took a friend along with him and, because he only had sideline passes, they watched the game from the playing field.

On one wild end run the whole Notre Dame backfield swarmed off the field over the sideline where Rice and his friend were virtually unprotected. The Irish backs swept right through Rice, who had fallen to his knees.

"It's worse than a cavalry charge," he said to his friend. "They're like a wild horse stampede." The thought occurred to him again in the press box at the Polo Grounds the next year and he ticked it off on his typewriter. That's how the phrase "Four Horsemen" was born.

There were seven other men on that 1924 Notre Dame team, and they too received their portion of national fame via a colorful nickname.

Who were the Seven Mules?

The linemen who paved the way for the "Four Horsemen" of the 1924 Notre Dame team were Ed Huntsinger and Charles Collins, ends; Joe Bach and Edgar (Rip)

Miller, tackles; Noble Kizer and John Weibel, guards, and Adam Walsh, center. The Seven Mules were good, but many people claim that they would have been no match for the line of the 1929 Fordham Rams.

The 1929 Fordham team had an undefeated season, winning seven and tying two. Its line yielded only 19 points in nine games! A caption writer seeking to describe a photo of these durable players gave it the title "Seven Blocks of Granite," and the name stuck.

Who were the Seven Blocks of Granite?

Actually some of the players on that team overlapped into the 1930 season, but the personnel of the two squads varied only slightly, so that 10 men got credit for being the Seven Blocks of Granite. They were Harry Kloppenburg and John Conroy, left ends; Francis Foley, left tackle; Walter Tracy and John Healy, left guards; Tony Siano, center; Pete Wisnieski, right guard; John Cannella and Mike Miskinis, right tackles; and Adam Elcewicz, right end.

The 1937 Fordham team also went undefeated in eight games, winning seven and tying one. They gave up only 16 points and once again the name was revived. Again there were more than seven men who got credit for being on the granite line. They included Henry Jacunski, Dick Healey and John Druze, ends; Albert Barbartsky, Paul Berezney, Ed Franco, Dul and Borzin, tackles; Michael Kochel, Vince Lombardi, Pierce and Marion, guards; and Alex (Woji) Wojciechowicz, at center.

Wisniewski, Wojciechowicz, Barbartsky and Franco were All-Americans.

I don't know why it is, but football fans don't seem to

be interested in the statistical side of the sport; they seem more interested in individual achievement or in great plays or great games. One of the reasons for this, I think, is that in some cases the statistics may be misleading. I mean who should get credit for the six points, the guy who plunges over from the two-yard line or the guy who ran it 80 yards to put it there in the first place? Another reason is that the figures get out of hand. A lifetime batting average or a home-run record are nice, tidy three-digit figure, whereas a player's total yards gained rushing runs into the thousands and doesn't mean too much when compared with someone else's (what's a few hundred yards more or less?).

But when it comes to individual achievement, that's something else again, and here the fans never tire of comparing their favorites. But there was one achievement by a football player that still has people shaking their heads.

Who once made four long touchdown runs in the first ten minutes of a game?

Harold ("Red") Grange, the Galloping Ghost of Illinois, turned in one of the greatest performances ever seen on an American gridiron against Michigan at Urbana, Illinois, on October 18, 1924.

The flashing, red-haired phenomenon, who had been named an All-American the previous year, thrilled a crowd of 67,000 in single-handedly routing the Wolverines, 39–14.

On the opening kickoff Grange tore through the Michigan eleven for 95 yards and a touchdown before the game was 10 seconds old. Before the Wolverines could recover from the shock Grange made their traumatic experience permanent with three more touchdown runs of 66, 55 and 40 yards. He even had time to leave the game to a thunderous ovation before the first period ended.

He returned in the third quarter and scored a fifth touchdown, on a 15-yard run, and in the fourth period he

passed 23 yards for Illinois' final score. In all, he handled the ball 21 times and gained 402 yards!

Grange was a baffling type runner who could untangle himself from clusters of would-be tacklers when it seemed he was hopelessly trapped. He was also a good blocker and tackler and an expert passer.

Midwestern football, as played in the rugged Big Ten, and the exploits of the Galloping Ghost had been heard of in the effete East, but all was taken with a grain of salt.

That is, until Grange hit Philadelphia on October 31, 1925, to face the Pennsylvania Quakers. The Eastern fans could not believe that Grange was as great as the stories coming out of the Midwest said he was.

Grange proved he was not a myth. Before 65,000 dumbfounded spectators, Grange dodged and slithered his way over a slippery, muddy field for three touchdowns as the Illini humbled the Quakers, 24–2.

Twice he went 60 yards for scores, leaving the Quaker team 40 yards behind him on one of the runs. His third scoring run was for 24 yards through a compact defense which he literally dragged along with him before he was hauled down from behind in the end zone. He carried the ball 36 times and gained 363 yards on a day when most runners would have been bogged down in the mud. Grange had left his mark on the City of Brotherly Love.

In his three-year college career Grange rushed for 3,637 yards and passed for 643 for a total of 4,280.

Which famous player could perform with equal skill at end, tackle and fullback?

Bronko Nagurski of Minnesota. A great many coaches rank him as the greatest player of all-time—an appellation that was also easily applied to Jim Thorpe and Red Grange as a well as a few dozen others.

But Nagurski was a rare bird. He was a star end, a star tackle and a crushing fullback who could pass, switching to those positions when the circumstances demanded that he fill the gap. When he went to stardom with the Chicago Bears of the pro league his name became a household word. "Who do you think you are? Nagurski!"

Another player of the same mold was Ernie Nevers of Stanford, a bruising fullback who virtually outplayed Notre Dame's "Four Horsemen" in the 1925 Rose Bowl game although Stanford was beaten, 27–10.

Football is one of the few sports in which coaches have gained some degree of the fame usually reserved for the players. Over the years, a handful of coaches have become legends in their own time.

Which coach has the best won-lost percentage in college football history?

You would be right if you said Knute Rockne of Notre Dame, but Frank Leahy, also of Notre Dame as well as Boston College, is a close second. Rockne's teams won 105 games, lost 12 and tied 5 for an .897 percentage (ties not included in figuring percentages), over a 13-year span from 1918 to 1930.

Leahy, also a coach for 13 years, compiled 107 victories, 13 defeats and 9 ties for a .892 percentage. Under Leahy, Notre Dame turned in a 39-game winning streak.

General Robert Neyland, over 21 years, turned in a record of 173–31–12—.848 for third place.

Knute Rockne, of course, was the most legendary coach in American football history. While his 13-year career as a mastermind of attack and defense came nowhere near matching the long tenures of Amos Alonzo Stagg, Pop Warner, Fielding Yost, Bob Zuppke and many other famous coaches, he captured the sporting world with his personality and color.

His untimely death in a plane crash in a Kansas cornfield on March 31, 1931, left a great void.

Which coach has won the most games?

Glenn S. ("Pop") Warner, who developed Jim Thorpe at Carlisle. He won 316 games, lost 104 and tied 32 for a .752 percentage. In victories he beat out Amos Alonzo Stagg, who had 311.

Warner was credited with inventing a number of today's basic formations. His career spanned 44 years and several schools, including Pittsburgh, Temple, Cornell and Stanford, where he produced three Rose Bowl teams.

Warner invented the crouch start, which is used generally now by all coaches, as well as the clipping block and the famous single and double wing backfield formations.

The Rose Bowl game was the forerunner of all the postseason bowl games we know today, but the first one was not called the Rose Bowl Game. Rather it had the lofty title of Tournament of Roses East-West Football Game.

Which two teams played in the first Rose Bowl game?

Michigan played Stanford in the first one on January 1, 1902. The Wolverines, led by Willie Heston, one of the great all-time backs, slaughtered the Indians, 49–0. The Michigan team, coached by Fielding H. Yost, who introduced the "point-a-minute" teams, had scored 550 points and stormed through 11 games undefeated, untied and unscored on before routing Stanford.

Heston was a marvel. In a four-year career he scored 93 touchdowns and 465 points.

How did the All-America Team originate?

Although there is some academic squabbling about it, Walter Camp of Yale is credited with starting the tradition of selecting the best 11 players throughout the country. He coached at Yale, while he was captain of the team, in 1878–1879, and at Stanford in 1892, 1894–1895. He was an adviser to Yale coaches from 1882 to 1910.

His first All-America Team appeared in 1889 and was dominated by the Big Three—Yale, Princeton and Harvard. Gradually Camp's selections grew wider in geographical scope and started to become truly representative of a national consensus.

Camp died in 1924 and Crowell-Collier, publishers of *Collier's Weekly*, continued the selections, with the aid of a board headed by Grantland Rice, for the next 21 years. In the meantime many other publications were also selecting their All-America Teams, as were the leading newspaper wire services. The practice continues today and the nation's fans look forward to it every fall.

What is the Heisman Trophy?

This is an annual award, given in honor of one of the game's great coaches, John W. Heisman, to the outstanding college football player in the United States. The first recipient, in 1935, was Jay Berwanger, a halfback at the University of Chicago. Mike Garrett, a University of Southern California halfback, won it in 1965.

The award is given each year by the Downtown Athletic Club of New York and although there are numerous other similar-type awards given throughout the nation, the Heisman is regarded as the most authoritative in picking the best player of the year.

For some reason football has lacked that inspired goofiness that has made baseball such an entertaining as well as interesting sport. Maybe it's because nobody on a football team has much time to stand around and trade insults with fans or think up practical jokes to play on his teammates the way some dotty outfielders do. But football has had its moments, and we'll conclude this chapter with one of the goofiest.

Who was the player who once ran 60 yards in the wrong direction in a Rose Bowl game?

Roy Riegels, the center and captain of the University of California's Golden Bears, became a football hero in reverse fashion for his wrong-way run in the 1929 Rose Bowl game. And there were 70,000 fans in the stands who witnessed it.

The wrong-way run turned out to be the decisive play of the game which Georgia Tech won, 8–7. In the second quarter, Riegels picked up a Tech fumble and started toward the Tech goal line. A platoon of Tech players sprung up in front of Riegels and, trying to get away from them, he cut back across the field.

Apparently he became confused and started toward his

own goal line, 60 yards away. Players from both sides stood amazed as he ran down the sidelines. Benny Lom, halfback for the Bears, sensed what was happening and took off after Riegels, who turned on more speed as he heard the pounding of feet behind him.

Finally Lom grabbed him at the three-yard line and spun him around, hoping to run interference for him in the right direction. But a swarm of Tech players nailed Riegels and drove him back to the one.

California went into punt formation, but Riegels at center, and Lom, who was to do the punting, were worn out and pretty nervous from their merry-go-round experience. The punt was blocked and the ball rolled out of the end zone. The officials ruled that a California man had touched the ball, however, and a safety, the margin of victory, was scored against the Golden Bears.

16

The Pros Have It

WHAT do you say about pro football that hasn't been said already? It's like being at a comedians' convention and having to tell the last story. There are so many stories about the fantastic growth and popularity of this sport that it's hard to know which one to start with. So . . .

Have you heard the one about the New York couple who were getting a divorce, and the husband and wife were amicably dividing up their possessions until they came to the question of who was to get title to the two season tickets to the Giants' games? They couldn't agree, so they decided to stop the divorce and remain married until the end of the season! And then there's the one about the businessman whose company transferred him from Chicago to New York. He advertised in the papers, seeking a fan who was moving to Chicago. He wanted to swap commodities—his Bears' tickets for Giants'.

The fanatical loyalty of pro football followers apparently knows no bounds or age limits. Vinnie Swerc, a

middle-aged executive from Staten Island, has been assisting the trainers in the Giants' locker room, toting the trays of water cups to the players during timeouts on the field and shagging the football after field-goal and extra-point attempts for more than 30 years—and at no pay—to be close to his favorites. Frank Keegan, now in his late sixties, has been performing similar duties for the Philadelphia Eagles for many seasons, again as a hobby.

Another is Abe Abraham, a Cleveland restaurateur, who is known as "The Man in the Brown Suit." Ever since the Browns were organized in 1946, he has helped out at the press gate and then, during the game, has been the "catcher" for Lou Groza's kicks. And, of course, he always wears a brown suit.

And would you believe that once the FBI alerted fans to be on the lookout for a man on its list of the "ten most

wanted fugitives." When an FBI agent was asked whether the public announcement wouldn't keep the criminal from attending a game, he said: "We doubt it. He likes pro football too much."

And how about the woman in Chicago who shot her husband because he wouldn't take her to a game?

Commonplace are the chartered buses and planes that carry groups of dedicated fans to the away games. One this season was from New York to Los Angeles for die-hard (and well-heeled) Giants' rooters at a cost of $388 per person! The trips are all the more remarkable because all that the fans have to do to watch their heroes is relax in their living rooms and see the away games for free on their television sets.

But as Al Jolson said, you ain't heard nothin' yet. If this were just the story of one league, the National Football League, then that would be enough in itself. But I've been through two expansions.

In 1949 I broadcast the games of the Buffalo Bills of the All America Conference. (I hesitate to admit it now . . . the team went out of business right afterwards.) You know how involved you can get with a ball club. Well, I was really involved with the Bills. I know I wasn't a "homer," but I was sure enough a rooter. When the N.F.L. had swallowed the earlier All America Conference, all Buffalo had left was a stadium. So when the new American Football League got going you were "Gung Ho" if you lived in Buffalo or anywhere an A.F.L. team was born. You can imagine my consternation when I got to New York and found out, via my radio show, that the A.F.L. hadn't quite "arrived."

It was as if I had come from another world. What made it seem so unbelievable was that there was an A.F.L. team in New York! It's all part of the past now, but I still laugh when I remember some of those early sessions on the air. Like the day I said I thought Cookie Gilchrist was a better all-around football player than Jimmy Brown. Mind you, I didn't say runner, I said all-around player. I felt then and I feel now that eleven Cookie Gilchrists would beat eleven Jimmy Browns. You don't agree? Well, neither do most of my listeners, and that's why I had more debates per day than any time since. The irony of the whole thing is that the year of peace between the two leagues saw Jimmy Brown retire to become a full-time actor and Cookie retire from the Denver team. But the game continues. It grows and grows and where it'll stop nobody knows.

If more proof is needed, the television contracts of both leagues spell out in dollars just how widespread and intense the interest is in pro football. The 1966 and 1967 National Football League regular-season games cost the Columbia Broadcasting System 37.6 million dollars! And the TV rights for the N.F.L. title game went to CBS for a cool four million dollars for two years—the highest price for a one-day sporting event. The A.F.L. insured its stability with a $36-million, five-year contract with the National Broadcasting Company.

Is it any wonder that pro football zealots proclaim that their sport has overtaken baseball as the national pastime?

The present eminence of pro football is a far cry from its early—and not so early—days of struggle and woe. It had to survive many disastrous seasons, when teams and franchises often appeared and disappeared from one fall to the next. How familiar are you with the early history of pro football?

THE PROS HAVE IT

Where and when was the first professional football game played?

The town of Latrobe, Pennsylvania, about 40 miles from Pittsburgh, earns the honor as the site of the first acknowledged pro game. Sponsored by the local Y.M.C.A., the game matched Latrobe against a team from the nearby town of Jeannette and was played on August 31, 1895. The home team won, 12–0, and the players were paid $10 each.

For the next 25 years the sport was concentrated mainly in Pennsylvania, Ohio, Indiana, Illinois and New York. Teams were casually organized, scheduling was an impromptu affair and the better players shifted to wherever the money beckoned. The pay was low, with few getting more than a hundred dollars a game. Many collegians played under pseudonyms on Sundays after their Saturday varsity efforts. Knute Rockne, after he was graduated from Notre Dame, was supposed to have set some sort of record by playing for six different teams in one season. "Pudge" Heffelfinger of Yale fame starred later on with a Pittsburgh team, and Glenn ("Pop") Warner was a guard on a Syracuse eleven that played in Madison Square Garden against the Philadelphia Nationals on December 28, 1902, and won, 6–0.

That same year Connie Mack organized his baseball Athletics into a football team and claimed the "world" championship after his club defeated Pittsburgh, 12–6. Pittsburgh had a fullback named Christy Mathewson, who had been a football standout at Bucknell and had just started his magnificent baseball career.

Heated rivalries sprang up among such Ohio towns as Canton, Akron, Massillon, Columbus and Dayton. The great Jim Thorpe began his pro career with Canton in 1915 (he was also a major-league outfielder for six seasons, but had trouble hitting the curve ball; lifetime average, .252) and was a terror for the next decade. He was a bruising back, but he also had the interesting custom of covering his shoulder pads with sheet metal, which made tackling him a memorable experience.

In the late 1910's such future coaching greats as Tuss McLaughry, Jock Sutherland and Earle ("Greasy") Neale banged heads on various Ohio teams.

By 1920 the time was thought to be at hand to try to organize the first pro football league. Named the American Professional Football Association, it was the forerunner of the National Football League. Eleven teams joined and the fee was a flat $100.

Who were the original teams in the first pro football league?

The teams were the Akron Professionals, the Dayton Triangles, the Cleveland Indians, the Canton Bulldogs, the Massillon Tigers, Rochester, N. Y., Rock Island, Ill., Muncie, Ind., Hammond, Ind., the Chicago Cardinals, and the Decatur, Ill., Staleys. The meeting took place in the office of Ralph Hays, an auto dealer, in Canton on September 17, 1920. For the value of his name Thorpe was elected president. However, by April of the next year the league had to be reorganized, and Joe Carr, a former sports writer and manager of a Columbus team, took over as president, a position he held with distinction until he died in 1939.

Three teams dropped out after that first season and five entered, including the Green Bay Packers, who eventually managed, despite periodic tribulations, to secure a unique niche in sports as the smallest town with a big-league franchise and as a community-owned enterprise, with stockholders pledged not to receive any dividends, all profits being plowed back into the club.

In 1922 the name of the league was officially changed to the National Football League, but the fortunes of the teams failed to improve appreciably through the 1920's. Red ink was the dominant color. Also in 1922 George Halas, who had been present at the founders' meeting, moved his Staleys to Chicago, and the Bears, Cardinals and Packers were to be the only survivors of the perilous early years of the league.

Which famous college player attracted the first great pro football crowds?

One brief spurt of prosperity occurred in 1925 when Harold ("Red") Grange, the nation's football hero for his exploits at Illinois, signed with the Bears and attracted sell-out crowds that season, including a mob (they broke down the gates and stormed into the Polo Grounds) estimated at 80,000 for his first New York appearance.

That game made a believer out of Tim Mara, who together with Will Gibson had paid $500 a few months earlier for the New York franchise. Mara, who knew nothing about pro football, was reported to have put up the money "because a New York franchise for anything should be worth $500." A lot of bleak years had to pass before Mara's opinion was justified.

Every year there were franchise shifts, additions and losses. The league had as many as 22 teams in 1926—probably the result of the turnouts for Grange the previous season—and as few as eight in the depression year of 1932.

The key year for pro football was 1933. The goal posts were put on the goal line, forward passing was legalized

from any spot behind the line of scrimmage and the league was divided into two divisions, with a championship playoff game between the divisional winners. The change in format and title game was proposed by George Preston Marshall, one of the new owners of the Boston Redskins.

297

Who invented the football draft system?

Bert Bell, then a co-owner of the Philadelphia Eagles, proposed in 1935 a system of drafting college seniors that was to form one of the foundations of success for the league in helping to keep the teams well-balanced. Bell's plan that the clubs should pick players in reverse order to their won-lost records of the previous season was adopted, and has been used ever since.

The league became relatively stable through the 1930's, with fewer franchise changes and a slowly greater acceptance by the public. Attendance figures inched upward from 492,684 in 1934 (the first year they were tabulated) until they hit the million mark for the first time in 1939.

After World War II, having persevered through depression and war, the National Football League looked forward to better times, only to find a rival league ready for battle—the All America Conference. The A.A.C. stayed in business for four years before tossing in the towel.

Who were the nine teams in the All America Conference?

The team you're most likely not to remember is the Miami Seahawks, who lasted only the first season before tossing in the towel. The other A.A.C. members were the Cleveland Browns, the Baltimore Colts, the Buffalo Bills, the Brooklyn Dodgers, the New York Yankees, the Chicago Rockets, the San Francisco 49ers and the Los Angeles Dons.

THE PROS HAVE IT

Competition between the two leagues for the top college stars drove salaries skyward (a situation that was repeated to an even higher degree between the N.F.L. and the A.F.L. until their truce) and proved too costly for the A.A.C. to continue operating after four seasons. The A.A.C. suffered from box-office miseries also in all cities except San Francisco, Cleveland, Buffalo and Baltimore, and was simply ahead of its time. TV revenues, non-existent then, might have made the difference.

On the field the A.A.C. caliber of play was comparable to the N.F.L., except that it was hurt competitively by the domination of the Browns and the organizational genius of Paul Brown.

The Cleveland Browns' four-year record in the All America Conference is almost unbelievable. In 54 regular-season games, they were beaten only four times and were tied only three times as against 49 victories as they won division and league titles all four years. They were undefeated in 1948.

Who was the great quarterback who led the Cleveland Indians to four straight A.A.C. championships?

Otto Graham, who has to be one of the great pro quarterbacks of all time. Graham had plenty of help from those great Cleveland teams, however. He had a fine blocker and running threat at fullback and two outstanding receivers. Marion Motley was the fullback and Mac Speedie and Dante Lavelli were the leading pass catchers.

After the A.A.C. folded, the Browns joined the N.F.L. together with the 49ers and the Colts—and Cleveland continued to demonstrate its class in the older league right from the start.

How many N.F.L. division titles did the Cleveland Browns win in a row?

Paul Brown's charges captured six successive crowns from 1950 to 1955 before the New York Giants finally prevailed in 1956. That also was the first season the Browns had to get along without the incomparable Graham, who had retired.

By the early fifties, the free substitution rule, which heralded the age of the specialist, was a permanent part of the game. The televising of games began and Bert Bell, who took over from Elmer Layden as commissioner, instituted a wise policy—let the fans see the away games on TV and black out the home games, making the fans come to the ballpark. The video exposure sparked the boom through the fifties.

Then the American Football League was born in 1960. Despite much red ink, horrible management of the New York Titans in the important "showcase" city and the relocation of two franchises (the Chargers from Los Angeles to San Diego, the Dallas Texans to the Kansas City Chiefs), the new league experienced much less travail than any previous organization and, thanks to TV money, was assured of survival. The merger with the N.F.L., which is to be completely realized by 1970, guarantees its rise to equal stature as a major league.

Thirty years after the first World Series, pro football started its own "world series" with the New York Giants and Chicago Bears meeting in the first championship

game. Only 26,000 fans were in Wrigley Field for that inaugural title clash on December 17, 1933. They saw a close game, the lead shifting back and forth five times, before the Bears pulled it out late in the final quarter with a bit of razzle-dazzle. Bronko Nagurski flipped a short pass from the Giant 36 to Bill Hewitt, who lateraled to Bill Karr, and he went the rest of the way for the deciding points in a 23–21 victory.

What was "the greatest football game ever played"?

Of all the spectacular title contests since 1933, one has earned the popular description of "the greatest game ever played"—the 1958 sudden-death overtime battle between the Giants and the Baltimore Colts, which made a living legend of Johnny Unitas. Most fans recall that a poised Unitas marched the Colts down the field in the last two minutes to set up the tying field goal and then, in the overtime, directed the drive for the winning touchdown. But how about some of the other fascinating details of that game?

The Giants were underdogs in the game—and for good reason. They were battered and tired after an injury-plagued season and an uphill climb to the Eastern Conference title. It had taken Pat Summerall's 49-to-51-yard (snow obscured the lines) field goal in the last few seconds to beat the Browns, 13–10, in the final game of the season and enable the Giants to tie Cleveland for the division title. Then they had shut out the Browns, 10–0, in the playoff game. In contrast, the Colts had breezed into the Western title and were well-rested. The fact that the Giants had beaten the Colts, 24–21, midway in the season was meaningless. Unitas had sat out the game with an injury, George Shaw taking over at quarterback, and as the Giants were to find out, there was a difference.

"The greatest game ever played" tag wouldn't describe the first half. Play was generally sloppy, with five fumbles, the Colts cashing in on one of Frank Gifford's two bobbles for their first touchdown. The Colts clearly had the upper hand and led, 14–3, at halftime.

Baltimore seemed ready to break the game open in the third period, moving to a first down on the Giant 3. But the gritty New York defenders, who had saved many a game through the year, refused to yield. Fullback Alan Ameche plunged to the one-yard line, but Unitas was stopped cold by Sam Huff & Co. on a quarterback sneak. Rosey Brown, an offensive tackle who was rushed in to bolster the defensive line, and Andy Robustelli held Ameche to no gain on the next play. Fourth down and still a yard to go. Unitas faked a handoff to Ameche and pitched to L. G. Dupre who tried to circle right end. Linebacker Cliff Livingston shook off a blocker and crashed through to nail Dupre for a four-yard loss.

The goal-line heroics put a spark into the Giants' attack. Three plays later Charley Conerly passed from the New York 13 to Kyle Rote, who was cutting over the middle. Rote eluded two Colts' secondarymen and raced down the right sideline. But he dropped the ball on the Baltimore 25! Alex Webster, trailing the play, scooped it up and got to the Baltimore one before being knocked out of bounds. The play gained 86 yards. Mel Triplett bulled over for the touchdown and the Giants were back in business.

The momentum was now with the Giants. Dick Modzelewski broke through to spill Unitas on the next sequence of plays. The crowd of 64,185 at Yankee Stadium, except

lor patches of Colts' fans, sent up another tremendous roar.

Don Maynard returned the Baltimore punt to the New York 19. After Webster gained three, Conerly connected with Bob Schnelker for 17 yards. The Giants' wiry old pro faked throwing twice and then passed to Schnelker in the clear at the Baltimore 30. Schnelker (good hands, no speed) was brought down on the Baltimore 15. Conerly faded back again, Gifford outfeinted a Colt cornerback and made up for his first-half errors, catching the pass on the three-yard line and going over with a Colt on his back.

In five minutes the Giants had turned the game around and were ahead, 17–14.

But the Colts came back. One drive stalled and a 46-yard field-goal try by Bert Rechichar was short. Then Baltimore received a break midway in the final period. Phil King fumbled a handoff and Ordell Braase recovered for Baltimore on the New York 42. The Colts moved to the 27. Second down and six. But Robustelli barreled in and smeared Unitas for an 11-yard loss. Then Modzelewski crashed through and tackled Unitas for a nine-yard loss back to the New York 47. Too far for a field-goal try. Ray Brown punted to Jimmy Patton and the Giants took over on their 19.

When Conerly completed a 10-yard toss to Webster for a first down on the New York 34, only about 3 minutes remained. Webster hit the line for a yard, then Gifford went off right tackle for five. Third down and four. One more first down and the Giants could run out the clock. Gifford tried to skirt right end. Gino Marchetti made the play of the game, fighting off two blockers and tackling Gifford a foot short of the first down! The play gave Baltimore a last chance and cost Marchetti a broken leg.

The Giants had to punt and Don Chandler spiraled a high one to Carl Taseff, who called for a fair catch on the Baltimore 14. Only 1:56 was left on the clock.

Unitas failed with two passes but clicked with Lenny Moore on the vital third-down play for 11 yards. After another incomplete pass, Unitas and Ray Berry, who caught 56 passes during the season and a TD aerial earlier in the game, teamed up. First, Berry broke over the middle for a pass, outfoxing his defender, Carl Karilivacz, and ran to midfield, a 25-yard advance. Only 64 seconds were left. Then Berry cut sharply and caught a 10-yarder. Next, Berry feinted Karilivacz to the inside, swerved to his left and grabbed a perfect peg from Unitas for 22 yards to the New York 13. Steve Myrha, the short-range field-goal kicker, hustled in and tied it up from the 20 as seven seconds showed on the clock! Unitas had done it!

Now the pendelum swung the other way. The Giants had given it their best shot, had been so close—and missed. They were down and the Colts were fired up. The finish of the first overtime period in a championship game seemed almost predictable. The Giants received the kick-off, were unable to advance and Baltimore took over on its own 20.

With time to spare, Unitas mixed up the attack between passes and runs and Baltimore moved steadily forward. Only once was there a temporary setback when Modzelewski smothered Unitas for an eight-yard loss. Unitas threw to Berry for 21 yards to the New York 43. On a draw play, Ameche ran for 23 more. Another pass to Berry gained 12 yards to the New York 8 for a first down. Unitas displayed his boldness two plays later by throwing to Jim Mutscheller, the right end, in the right flat, a dangerous play that close to the goal line, for the ball could easily be picked off with a clear route for a touchdown. With the ball on the one Ameche burst over right guard on third down at 8:15 and the Colts owned a historic 23–17 triumph.

Some post-mortem comments were critical of Unitas for risking a fumble and not calling for a field goal from that close up, which would have been almost as automatic as an extra-point attempt. The Baltimore rejoinder was that the Colts had one down left if Ameche hadn't scored.

THE PROS HAVE IT

What was satisfying about the Giants-Colts sudden-death overtime battle?

After the game, players and fans alike expressed satisfaction over the fact that both teams had had a chance to score. If the Giants, who won the toss to receive, had driven to a touchdown, the game would have ended—and the arguments begun. Think of all the broken friendships, the high blood pressure, the ulcers, the pure despair that were avoided! As it is, one remembers the game fondly.

The N.F.L. had the first overtime championship game but the A.F.L. owns the distinction of having the longest championship game, with the game not decided until a second extra period.

Which two teams played the longest pro championship game?

The Dallas Texans and the Houston Oilers in the 1962 A.F.L. title game. After the Texans ran up a 17–0 lead in the first two quarters, the Oilers, with the veteran George Blanda at the helm, came back in the second half and evened the score, Blanda converting after Charlie Tolar's one-yard buck early in the final period.

When the quarter ended in a 17–17 deadlock, halfback Abner Haynes, the Dallas offensive captain, went to midfield for the coin toss. Haynes was instructed by Coach Hank Stram to pick the end of the field with the wind advantage. Haynes won the toss, but surprisingly said: "We'll kick." So Dallas lost both the advantage of receiving and the wind.

The unintended edge did not help the Oilers to score and the Texans were similarly frustrated through the first 15-minute overtime period, but they had the ball as the period ended.

At the beginning of the second extra period, Len Dawson completed a 10-yard pass to halfback Jack Spikes and Spikes raced for 19 yards to the Houston 19. Rookie Tommy Brooker became the Dallas hero of the day by kicking a 25-yard field goal at 2:58 and the Texans won, 20–17.

THE PROS HAVE IT

309

Which player has scored the most points in a N.F.L. title game?

Paul Hornung of the Green Bay Packers scored 19 points against the New York Giants in the 1961 championship game. As the Packers routed the Giants, 37–0, Hornung, who was on furlough from his military service, tallied just about every way possible except for a safety. He made the opening touchdown on a six-yard run, booted three field goals of 17, 22 and 19 yards, and kicked four conversion points.

What were the two lowest scores of N.F.L. championship games?

Low-scoring games are the exception in N.F.L. title games, yet the Philadelphia Eagles had two successive shutouts, beating the Chicago Cardinals, 7–0, in 1948 and the Los Angeles Rams, 14–0, in 1949! The first game took place in a snowstorm at Shibe Park, and the weather made a mockery of both offenses. A Cardinal fumble recovered by Frank Kilroy on the Chicago 17 in the fourth period paved the way for the game's only touchdown, with Steve Van Buren scoring through the snow from the five.

The next year the Eagles faced the Rams in the Los Angeles Coliseum. A heavy rain hampered Los Angeles' feared aerial attack, directed by Bob Waterfield, while the Eagles, relying on Van Buren, slogged along the ground to win, 14–0. Still, a 31-yard pass from Tommy Thompson to Pete Pihos accounted for the first Philly touchdown.

Miserable weather has played a part in many N.F.L.

championship games, but in one the winning team turned it to its advantage.

Which teams participated in the "sneakers game"?

The New York Giants defeated the Chicago Bears in the 1934 championship game, which has been known ever since as the "sneakers game." On an icy Polo Grounds field the Giants were slipping and sliding to defeat in the first half. They were behind, 10–3, at intermission when they were told in the locker room to put on basketball sneakers that had been obtained by a trainer from the Manhattan College gym. With the benefit of superior footing the Giants outplayed the Bears in the second half

and were victorious, 30–13, Ken Strong running for two touchdowns in a 27-point fourth quarter.

In pro football, the name of the game is quarterback, the premier position on the team. You're probably familiar with the exploits and the backgrounds of famous passers, but let's see if you can identify them.

Who has been called "the perfect play-caller"?

Sid Luckman of the Chicago Bears. The accolade as the perfect play-caller came from the Bears' coach George Halas, who said that Luckman never called the wrong play in 12 years of pro football!

Luckman made it in pro football the hard way. He was a schoolboy star at Erasmus Hall High School in Brooklyn, but instead of enrolling at a college football powerhouse, where his talents would be properly displayed, he picked Columbia, which had a wonderful coach in Lou Little but not much in the way of material. Luckman took a beating playing with the outmanned Lions (he had his nose broken three times), but Halas' shrewd eye picked him out, even in a losing game. Sid proved to be the right choice and became the first great pro T quarterback as Halas refined and polished up the old formation. He was a deft ballhandler and a master at faking, and led the Bears to four world championships. With such runners as Bill Osmanski, George McAfee, Ray Nolting and Joe Maniaci, Luckman didn't have to throw as often as most of the other passers. But he still shares the record for most touchdown passes (7) in one game.

Luckman is probably best remembered as the field general of the 1940 Bears championship team.

What was the highest score of a N.F.L. championship game?

The Chicago Bears creamed the Washington Redskins, 73–0, in the 1940 championship match. The man at the controls, of course, was Sid Luckman, who had to play only the first half.

Who is usually rated the greatest quarterback of all time?

It has to be Slingin' Sammy Baugh. They say that when he first came up with the Washington Redskins, he was told to hit the receiver in the eye—and he asked which

eye! Although he had gotten off to a slow start in college
—he couldn't make the first team at Texas Christian University until his junior year—his rookie season as a pro

was sensational. He not only led his team into the title game, but he was also the star, pitching three touchdown passes! That rookie season of 1937 was the beginning of a fabulous career that covered 16 years. He was considered the most accurate of all the passers in the league and he could throw long or short equally well and modify the speed of the pass to suit the receiver and the situation. As a punter he was the league's best five times, and one season he led the league in interceptions—the other fellows'! Incidentally, his nickname didn't stem from his skill with a football. He was tagged Slingin' Sammy as a young third baseman for the way he fired the ball to first.

Which famous quarterback was cut by his first pro team?

The Pittsburgh Steelers pulled the boner of all time when they dropped Johnny Unitas, a ninth-round draft choice from the University of Louisville, before he even got into an exhibition game in 1955. One of the coaches said he was too dumb for pro football! Keith Molesworth, director of playing personnel for the Baltimore Colts, spotted Unitas's name on a list of free agents while searching for a back-up man for quarterback George Shaw and made a 65-cent phone call to his home in Pittsburgh. Unitas was strictly a bench-warmer until a knee injury to Shaw in the 1956 season gave him his big chance. He made his debut against the Bears, and was not exactly a sensation. He was intercepted four times as Chicago routed the Colts, 58–27. But he came on strong the following game and has been Baltimore's man with the golden arm ever since.

Which famous quarterback nearly quit pro football after five unsuccessful seasons?

Charley Conerly of the New York Giants. After a splendid career at Mississippi, Charley was picked by the Washington Redskins, but with the seemingly ageless Sammy Baugh on the premises, and with the recent draft-choice Harry Gilmer, the All-American from Alabama, due to arrive any minute, owner George Marshall considered Conerly expendable and traded him to the Giants for two backs, Howie Livingston and Pete Stout.

After his rookie year in New York in 1948, Conerly, strictly a single-wing man at Ole Miss, had to learn the T when the Giants decided to scrap Steve Owen's A formation. To teach Charley, the Giants hired as backfield coach the young but brainy Allie Sherman, a left-handed thrower from Brooklyn College whose big-time pro experience consisted basically of sitting on the bench for a few years in Philadelphia.

The Giants had poor clubs through the early 1950's and Conerly absorbed much punishment, both on the field from the players and off the field from the booing fans. "Go home, Charley" was a common banner at the Polo Grounds in those days. Conerly decided to quit after the 1953 season, but the new head coach, Jim Lee Howell, tracked him down to his cotton farm in Mississippi and persuaded him to return, promising him better protection up front. Howell kept his promise and Conerly blossomed into one of the game's great passers in the next eight years. One of Conerly's fortes was the ability to throw the ball away so cleverly when his receivers were covered that he never incurred a penalty for grounding the ball.

Who was the greatest pass receiver in pro football history?

Don Hutson of the Green Bay Packers is universally acclaimed as the greatest receiver in pro football history. He was invariably covered by two defenders, but that seldom stopped the elusive, sure-handed Hutson from catching passes. Twice he was voted the most valuable player in the league and he occupies a firm place on every all-time all-pro eleven. Playing in the days of one-platoon, 60-minute football, he also starred defensively at halfback and as a field-goal kicker, leading the N.F.L. in that specialty in 1943. During his 11 seasons from 1935 to 1945, he was a major factor in the Packers' winning three world championships.

The specialized techniques of two-platoon football have enabled a few receivers to erase a number of records that Hutson, who once held them all, had set. However, the brilliant Packers' end still dominates the record book with five entries.

Hutson led the league in pass receptions the most seasons (8), the most consecutive seasons (5) and the most consecutive games (95). He also holds the record for the most touchdown passes caught (100), and shares the mark for the most touchdown passes in one season (17) with Elroy Hirsch of the Los Angeles Rams.

A while back I maintained that football lacked that inspired wackiness which seems to characterize baseball. Well, I must admit that pro football has had its moments:

Who or what is a "Steagle"?

Steagle is the name derived from the merger of the Pittsburgh Steelers and the Philadelphia Eagles during the war year of 1943. (Question: Why wasn't it "Ealer"?) It is also the title of a recent novel by Irvin Faust, who used the name to characterize his hero (or anti-hero, if I remember the Steagles), a man who was neither one thing nor another, I take it.

That's the way to end a book. Plug somebody else's. Good talkin' to you! It's been a pleasure.